Reading for Meaning

On We Go

THIRD EDITION

PAUL McKEE · M. LUCILE HARRISON
ANNIE McCOWEN · ELIZABETH LEHR

HOUGHTON MIFFLIN COMPANY • Boston
NEW YORK • ATLANTA • GENEVA, ILL. • DALLAS • PALO ALTO

Stories that you will find:

Acknowledgment is hereby made to J. B. Lippincott Company, publishers, for permission to adapt the story Noodle by Munro Leaf. Copyright, 1937, by Munro Leaf.

STORIES
FOR YOU

Noodle

Once there was a little dog named Noodle, who was very long from front to back and very short from top to bottom.

Just a short way from Noodle's home there was a big garden. Noodle liked to dig in that garden. Almost every day he could dig up something that was good to play with or that was good to eat.

Digging in the garden was hard work for Noodle. Everything came back and hit him. That was because he was so long from front to back and so short from top to bottom.

One day Noodle began to dig deep down
into the garden. He was sure he would
find a bone there. In a little while all
you could see was the tip of his tail.
You couldn't even see his short back legs.

But Noodle kept on digging. Soon
you could not see even the tip of his tail.
Noodle knew a bone was not far away.

All at once his front feet hit
something hard. It was a bone.

Noodle began to dig faster. "I wish
I were not so long from front to back
and so short from top to bottom," he said.

Just then Noodle heard the sound of wings above him. He thought that maybe a bird had come to watch him, but he did not look to see. He went on digging in the hole.

Soon Noodle had the bone in his mouth. Then he turned himself around and came part way out of the hole. He put the bone down and looked around the garden for something with wings.

There was no bird anywhere, but there was a little white dog with wings just like a bird's. That was what Noodle had heard while he was digging in the hole.

The little white dog with wings was not so long from front to back as Noodle, and she was not so short from top to bottom. But she had a very short tail.

She smiled at Noodle.

"Who are you?" asked Noodle, wagging his tail, which was still down in the hole.

"I'm the dog fairy," she said, wagging her tail. "Didn't you hear my wings?"

"Yes," said Noodle. "I thought a bird had come to watch me dig. Would you like some of this good bone that I just found in this hole?"

"No, thank you," said the dog fairy. "It isn't very clean. I just came to the garden to give you your wish."

"What wish?" asked Noodle, still wagging his tail but looking a little hurt.

"The one that you made just as you found that wishbone," said the fairy.

9

"Why, so it is a wishbone!" said Noodle. "I forget — did I wish something when I was down in that hole? What was it?"

"You wished to be some other size and shape than you are," said the fairy. "You shall have your wish. What size and shape do you want to be?"

"I'm not sure right now," said Noodle. "May I have time to think about it?"

"Yes," said the fairy. "I'll come back to the garden tonight. Then you must tell me what size and shape you want to be."

Off she went on her white wings. For a little while Noodle kept on wagging his tail. Then he looked for the bone. It was gone!

"She took the wishbone with her!" said Noodle in surprise. He stopped wagging his tail. He wanted that bone!

Noodle came out of the hole and sat down. He could always think better that way.

"What size and shape would be good for me?" he asked himself.

"I know what I'll do!" he said. "I'll ask the animals at the zoo. They will know what size and shape I should be."

So off he went. Pitter, pitter, patter, patter, pitter, patter. That was the way his feet sounded when he was in a hurry.

His legs were so short he could not go very fast, but on he went, pitter, pitter, patter, patter, pitter, patter.

Now his tail was wagging again.

11

TO THE ZOO

Will Noodle Get Help at the Zoo?

It was a fine day. All the zoo animals
were out of doors. The zebra was
the first one that Noodle saw. He went
right up to the zebra — pitter, patter.

"Good morning, Mr. Zebra," Noodle said,
wagging his tail.

"Good morning, Noodle," said Mr. Zebra.
"What brings you here this fine day?"

"I have a question," said Noodle.

"Ask it," said Mr. Zebra.
"Ask any question you want to. Ask me
a hard one. I like questions."

"What's the best size and shape
for an animal to be?" asked Noodle.

"That's not a hard question," said
Mr. Zebra. "My size and shape is best."

"Why?" asked Noodle.

"I don't know — it just is best!"
said the zebra.

"Is it good for digging up bones
in the garden?" asked Noodle.

"I don't really know," said Mr. Zebra.
"I don't dig for bones. But it's fine
for pulling wagons."

"Do you pull wagons?" asked Noodle.

"No, but I'd like to," said Mr. Zebra.

"Why don't you, then?" asked Noodle.

"Look at my stripes," said Mr. Zebra. "You see I have two kinds. The black ones can be seen best in the daytime, and the white ones can be seen best at night."

"But I can't see why you don't pull wagons if you want to," said Noodle. "What do your stripes have to do with it?"

"I don't get time," answered Mr. Zebra. "I have to stand around all the time to let people look at me."

"That's too bad," said Noodle. "But I don't want to pull wagons anyway. I want to dig for bones in the garden. Your size and shape would not be best for me.

But thank you for telling me. Now I must run along. Good-by, Mr. Zebra."

"Good-by, Noodle," answered Mr. Zebra.

Away trotted Noodle on his short legs,
wagging his tail and thinking what
a fine day it was for digging in the garden.

"I'll ask somebody else to answer
my question," he said to himself.

As Noodle trotted on he saw Miss Ostrich.
That is, he saw all of her but her head.
That was in a hole in the sand.

"Good morning, Miss Ostrich," he called.

Out came Miss Ostrich's head in a hurry!
She looked very much surprised.

"Good morning, Noodle," she said.
"How did you know I was here?"

"I saw you," answered Noodle.

"You saw me!" cried Miss Ostrich.
"That's funny! I couldn't see you.
I don't understand it at all."

Noodle didn't wait to ask his question.
He was sure Miss Ostrich didn't know
anything about the best size and shape
for digging holes in gardens.

He just said, "Good-by!" and trotted off.

"What a silly dog!" said Miss Ostrich
as she put her head into the hole again.

Noodle knew that it was almost time
for dinner and he didn't want to miss it.
But he wanted to get his question answered
once more before dinner. So he trotted
along faster until he saw Mr. Giraffe.

Mr. Giraffe was eating a fine dinner
from the top of a tree.   He could do that
because he had a very long neck.

"Good morning, Mr. Giraffe," said Noodle.

"Good morning," answered Mr. Giraffe.
"What brings you here at dinner time?"

"I have a question to ask," said Noodle.
"Won't you please stop eating?"

"I guess so," answered Mr. Giraffe, and
down came his long neck and head.
"But hurry up with your question.
I'm too hungry to wait long."

"My question is short," said Noodle.
"What's the best size and shape to be?"

"Mine is!" answered Mr. Giraffe.
"This neck is just fine for getting
dinners from tops of trees."

"Would your neck be fine for digging up
bones for dinner?" Noodle asked.

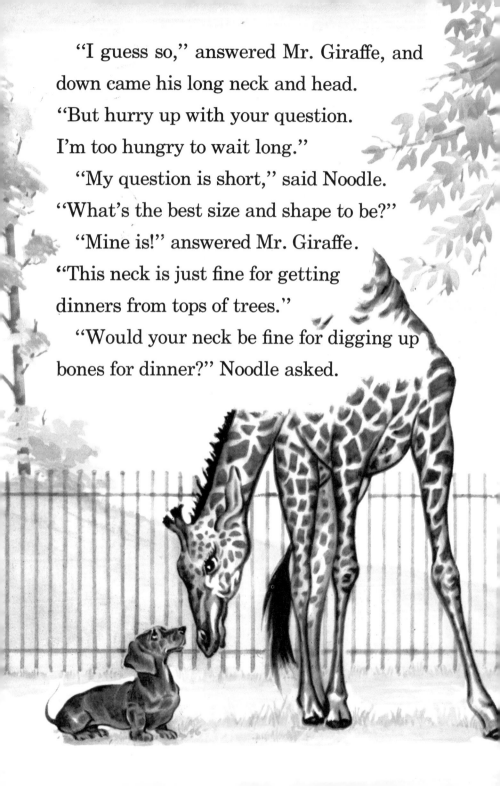

Mr. Giraffe laughed and laughed.

"What a silly question!" he cried.
"Who wants to dig up bones for dinner?"

"I do!" answered Noodle. "I want to dig
in the garden for bones for my dinner."

"That's just silly!" said Mr. Giraffe.

"No, it isn't," said Noodle. "I'm going
home for dinner right now. I get hungry
just thinking about bones. Thank you
for answering my question."

"Isn't it too bad!" thought Noodle
as he went trotting along. "A giraffe
can't dig up bones! What a neck! I know
I don't want a size and shape like his."

19

Noodle Goes Home

Pitter, patter, pitter, patter, pitter
went Noodle's feet as he trotted home
on his short legs. He wasn't happy.
His tail was not wagging. He was hungry and
getting hungrier at every pitter patter.

How silly all the zoo animals were,
he thought. But how could they know
the best size and shape for digging holes?
Not one of them liked to dig holes.

Noodle knew that he wanted to dig.
He didn't want to pull wagons around.
He didn't need a neck like a giraffe's.
He wasn't silly enough to put his head
down into the sand as Miss Ostrich did.

Noodle was afraid he couldn't think
of the right size and shape before night.

But he was too hungry to think any longer.
He got his dinner. Then he found a good
place in the garden and went sound asleep.

Noodle was still asleep when night came.
The first thing he heard was the sound
of wings.   The fairy was right above him.

"I have come back to give you your wish,"
she said almost in a whisper.

"So I see," said Noodle, but he didn't
see at all.   It was dark and he was still
almost asleep.

"Well, I'm waiting," said the fairy.
"What size and shape do you want to be?"

"I'm thinking," answered Noodle
as he stood up and stretched himself.

Noodle stretched himself again. "I want to keep the size and shape that I have now," he said, wagging his tail. "Does that surprise you, Miss — Miss Fairy?"

"Not at all," said the fairy. "Dogs and people are too much alike. They are always wishing for things that they really don't want. All fairies know that."

Off she went on her white wings.

"I guess I'd better not make any more silly wishes," said Noodle.

Then he took another good stretch and went back to sleep.

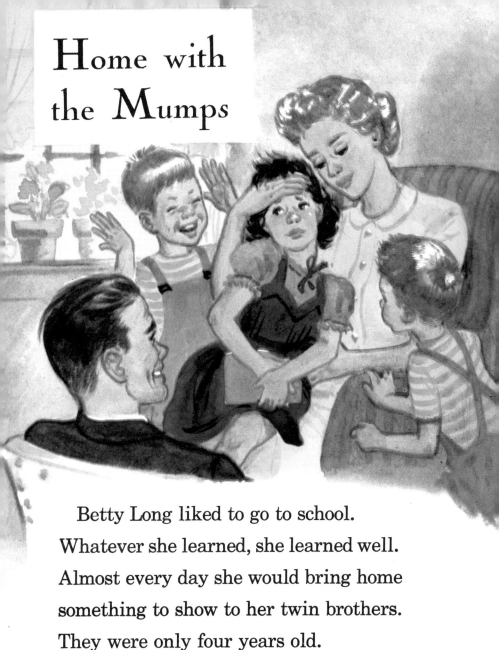

Home with the Mumps

Betty Long liked to go to school.
Whatever she learned, she learned well.
Almost every day she would bring home
something to show to her twin brothers.
They were only four years old.

One day Betty came home from school
with a big surprise. She had the mumps.

"Well!" said Mr. Long when he saw Betty.
"I know you like to learn everything,
but why did you learn the mumps?
I didn't have to learn mumps at school."

"I didn't learn the mumps," said Betty.
"I caught them from Ann."

"Caught them!" said Mr. Long, smiling.
"If I were going to catch something,
I'd try to catch something I wanted."

The twins, Bob and Bill, laughed.
They thought the mumps looked funny.

"Are mumps hard to catch?" Bob asked.

"Just wait!" cried Betty. "You'll have
twin mumps and you'll not laugh."

24

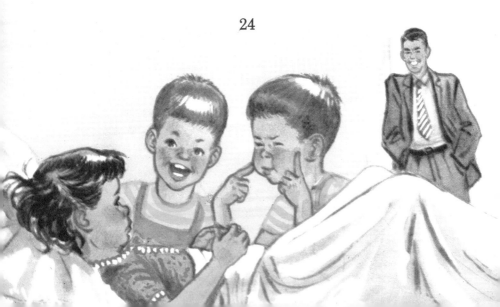

Because they were twins, Bob and Bill
were twice as sure of things as Betty was.

"We won't get the mumps," said Bob.

"We'll catch something good," said Bill.

"Wait and see," said Betty.

Betty was soon well enough to have
breakfast with Bob and Bill. One morning
they were having oranges. All at once
Bob and Bill began to cry.

"My neck hurts!" said Bob.

"My neck hurts too!" said Bill.

"Mumps!" cried Betty, trying not to smile.
"You'll have them twice as hard as I did."

"Will we, Mother?" Bob asked.

"I hope not," Mrs. Long said. "Eat
your breakfast now. Then go up to bed.
That is the best place for boys with mumps."

"I don't want any breakfast," said Bill.

Taking care of the twins was twice as hard
as taking care of Betty. Mrs. Long had
to run up and down the stairs many times
that day. One twin or the other wanted
something or was crying all the time.

When night came the twins' faces
and necks were twice as big as
they had been in the morning. Mrs. Long
was up twice as many times with the boys
as she had been with Betty.

Before breakfast she ran upstairs
to see about them.   Then she ran downstairs
to get breakfast and upstairs to take it
to them.   So it went all day.
By night time she was all tired out.

26

When Mr. Long came home, Mrs. Long said, "You'll have to sleep upstairs. I've put the twins in your bed downstairs."

"Fine!" said Mr. Long. "I've wanted to sleep upstairs sometime. I'll put the twins' beds end to end and have a bed that is really long enough for me."

"You'll have to put part of you in Bob's bed and part in Bill's," said Betty.

"I don't care!" said Mr. Long. "Mother can take better care of the twins if they sleep beside her downstairs. She won't have to carry hot cocoa and other things up and down the stairs all day long."

27

Breakfast Troubles for Daddy

Day by day the twins got better.

The mumps didn't hurt them so much now.

But they still took so much care that

Mrs. Long had more work than she could do.

One morning when Mr. Long

came downstairs, breakfast wasn't ready.

The cocoa wasn't made. The oatmeal

wasn't ready. Nothing was on the table.

He opened the bedroom door just enough

to look in. Mrs. Long looked at him

and tried to smile, but she was too tired.

"Don't get up!" said Mr. Long.

"I've thought of a way to help you.

I'll stay home today. I'll take care

of the twins and do the housework.

You go upstairs and stay in Betty's bed

all day. I'll take care of everything."

"They are twice as much trouble too,"
said Mrs. Long. "You'll have to work
twice as hard. They are hungry all the time.
They will want something all day long."

"I've taken care of them before," said
Mr. Long. "I know it will be more fun
to stay at home than to work all day."

Mrs. Long went upstairs and
was soon sound asleep in Betty's bed.

Mr. Long got dressed and went
to the kitchen to begin getting breakfast.
He put oatmeal and hot water into a pan
and turned on the burner under the pan.

Then he went into the twins' room.

"How about oatmeal and toast
for breakfast?" Mr. Long asked.
"And hot cocoa to drink?"

"That's fine!" answered Bill. "But
don't put much sugar in the oatmeal."

"Or in the cocoa," said Bob.
"Sugar makes mumps hurt."

"Make light brown toast," said Bill.

"Make twice as much as Mother does,"
said Bob.

"All right," said Mr. Long. "You stay
in bed, and I'll bring you your breakfast."

Just then Betty called, "Daddy! Daddy!
Come to the kitchen! Something is burning!"

Mr. Long hurried to the kitchen. He saw
that some of the oatmeal had run all over
the burner. He took the pan off the burner
and put oatmeal into two dishes.

Then he put some toast in the toaster
and took the oatmeal to the twins.

"Here you are! Eat this while I make
your toast and cocoa," said Mr. Long.

"Your oatmeal isn't like Mother's,"
said Bob. "See, I can drink it
right out of the dish."

"May we have our goldfish to play with
while you make the cocoa and toast?"
asked Bill. "We haven't seen our goldfish
for a long time. Put them between us."

Mr. Long put the glass jar
with the goldfish in it between the twins.

"Now don't tip it over," he said.

Just then Betty called, "Daddy!
Come here! The toast is burning!"

Mr. Long got to the kitchen quickly, but
the toast was burned black. He burned
his hand getting it out of the toaster.
Betty had to take care of his hand
before he could make more toast.

"Taking care of the twins is hard work,"
he said. "They keep me running
between the kitchen and the bedroom."

"Where's our cocoa?" Bob called.
"Won't you drink milk?" asked Mr. Long.
"No! We want cocoa," answered Bill.
Mr. Long put some milk into a pan, but
before he could put the pan on a burner,
Bob called again.
"Daddy! Come quickly!" he cried.
"Our goldfish are jumping around in bed!"
With the pan of milk in his hand,
Mr. Long ran into the bedroom. He caught
the goldfish as quickly as he could and
began to put them back into the jar.

There was no water in it. So he put
the goldfish into the pan of milk.

Then he thought that milk might not be
good for goldfish. So he ran
to the kitchen and put them into water
as quickly as he could.

Before he finished breakfast, he got
the twins up and made the bed up clean.

"No more goldfish in bed," he said as he
finished the work. "Get back into bed
and stay there while I finish making
some cocoa for us to drink."

Mr. Long had no more trouble getting breakfast. The children had all the cocoa they could drink and all the toast they wanted. After they had finished their breakfast, Mr. Long began to eat his.

As he was drinking his cocoa, he remembered something that made him smile. He had made the cocoa with the milk that the goldfish had been in.

He let Blackfeet, the kitten, finish drinking the cocoa. Blackfeet thought it was a very fine drink.

Then Bill called from the bedroom. "Mother reads a story to us every morning. Will you read us a story about Indians?"

"Yes, I will," said Mr. Long. "I've finished eating breakfast. I'll get a headdress and let you paint me up as a big chief. How does that sound?"

"Fine!" said all the children.

Bob put the Indian headdress on Mr. Long.

New Troubles

Betty got some paints and a pan of water.
Bill painted red stripes on Mr. Long's face.

Mr. Long looked so funny that the twins
began to laugh. Then they cried because
laughing made the mumps hurt so much.

Mr. Long sat down between the twins and
began to read, but he didn't read long.
Soon Bill tipped over the pan
of red paint water and got the bed wet.

"You'll have to get into Mother's bed,"
said Mr. Long. "I can't take time to make
this bed up clean twice in one day."

Mr. Long finished the story as quickly
as he could. Then he and Betty went
into the kitchen. They did the dishes and
cleaned up the oatmeal on the burner.

"You give the goldfish something to eat,
and I'll throw out this burned toast,"
said Mr. Long. "That will finish the work."

"You'll have to milk Sally,"
said Betty. "Can you milk a goat?"

"I've never seen a goat I couldn't milk,"
said Mr. Long. "I won't have any trouble
milking our good little Sally."

Mr. Long got a rope.   He put one end
of it around Sally's neck and
the other end around a post.   Then he tried
to milk the goat.

Sally would not let him milk her.   She
jumped around, pulled the rope off the post,
and ran away.   Mr. Long ran after her.

Just as he got hold of the rope, Sally
turned and ran between his legs.   Then she
ran around and around him.   Down he went
with the rope all around his feet and legs.

"Stop her!   Hold her!" he cried.
"Don't let her cut my legs off!"

Betty helped to hold Sally while Mr. Long
got the rope off his legs.   One leg had
a little cut on it.   Betty took care of that.

"Put on a dress, Daddy," said Betty.
"Then maybe Sally will let you milk her.
She has never been milked by a man."

"How silly!" he said. "But I'll try it."

He put on a dress and got a hat
with flowers on it. He didn't know that
it was Mrs. Long's best hat. The dress was
too short. He looked very silly
with the red Indian stripes on his face.

As soon as Mr. Long began to milk Sally,
he took off the hat and put it down.
Sally liked flowers. So, once in a while
she helped herself to a flower.

Mr. Long finished milking the goat,
put on the hat, and went to the kitchen.
Just then the bakery man came along.

When the bakery man saw Mr. Long
at the kitchen door, he wanted to run away.
At first he just stood with his mouth open.
Then he said, "Good morning, Miss. Do you
want to buy anything today?"

"Just a cake," said Mr. Long. "One
with very little sugar on it, please.
Sugar makes the mumps hurt very much.

And I'll thank you not to call me Miss.
I put on this dress and this hat
with flowers on it just to please Sally."

The bakery man didn't understand that,
but he asked no questions. He left a cake
and hurried back to his truck. All the way
he kept looking back at Mr. Long.

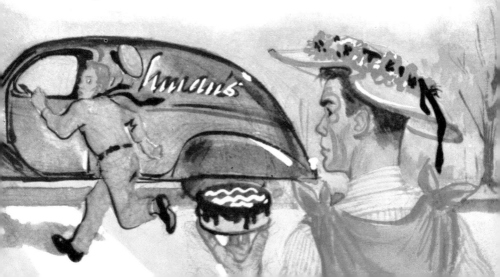

Mr. Long took off the hat and looked
at it. "I hope Sally liked the flowers,"
he said.

"Shall I clean the Indian stripes
off your face?" Betty asked.

"No, thank you," said Mr. Long. "I don't
really care about them. I think I'll
just stretch out on the twins' bed a while."

"You look funny, Daddy!" the twins said,
and they began to laugh. Laughing hurt
their mumps so much they began to cry.

Mr. Long put his arm over his face.
Just then Mrs. Long came downstairs.

40

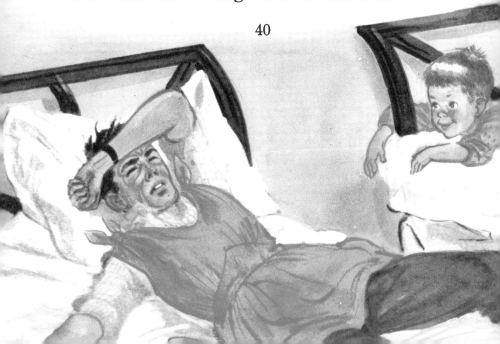

"What happened!" she cried.

"Nothing much," said Betty, as she came in from the kitchen. "Daddy had a little trouble with the breakfast and the goldfish and the goat. Everything is all right now.

I'm taking care of the twins and Daddy. I'm sure Daddy will be all right tomorrow."

Snipp and His Brothers

Once there were three brothers
who looked so much alike that no one
in town was ever sure which was which.

At times not even their mother
could tell them apart.

The three boys went everywhere together
and almost always did the same things.
But once in a while each one wanted to do
something different. Then they had
a hard time doing anything at all.

One brother was named Snipp, one was
named Snapp, and the third was named Snurr.

One morning Snipp, Snapp, and Snurr
were standing in front of their house.
All three wanted to go for a walk, but
each one wanted to go to a different place.

As they stood there talking, Mrs. Bunch
from next door came along.

"Good morning, Snipp, Snapp, and Snurr,"
she said. "Where are you going
this fine morning?"

"Good morning to you," said the boys.
"We want to go for a walk.
The trouble is that each of us
wants to go to a different place."

"You look so fine all dressed up
in your red suits that you really
should go somewhere," said Mrs. Bunch.
"Maybe I can help you get started.

I am going to give each of you
some money. Take the money and go
to the bakery.

If the baker has a big cake, buy it
and have him cut it into three big pieces
so that each of you can have a piece.
Or buy anything else that you want.

Now do you want to go different places?"

"Not now!" cried Snipp, Snapp, and Snurr
as they started away. Then they stopped.

"Thank you, Mrs. Bunch!" they said.

The boys started walking again.

"I'd like a piece of cake," said Snipp.

"Sometimes the baker has gingerbread cookies," said Snapp. "Cookies are better than pieces of cake."

"Let's find out what different things the baker has," said Snurr.

The three brothers hurried down the street to the bakery.

"Good morning, boys!" said the baker as they came into the bakery. "What can I do for you?"

"Mr. Baker, we have some money," said Snipp. "Have you any cake?"

"Mr. Baker, I don't want a piece of cake," said Snapp. "I want some gingerbread cookies."

"I don't want a piece of cake or some cookies," said Snurr. "I'd like a gingerbread man with sugar eyes."

"I see that each of you wants something different," said the baker.

"My gingerbread is very good. I have just started some new gingerbread batter. Come into the kitchen. You may watch me finish it. Then I'll bake a gingerbread man with sugar eyes for each of you.

I am going to bake some gingerbread cookies, too. They will be different sizes and different shapes. You may each have one of them."

"Will you bake some gingerbread men
with yellow sugar hair?" asked Snipp.

"And bake them with eyes?" asked Snapp.

"Can the eyes be blue like ours?"
asked Snurr.

"Yes! I'll make gingerbread men
with yellow sugar hair and blue sugar eyes,"
said the baker. "Climb up on this box
and watch me finish the batter."

"A gingerbread man like that will be
better than a piece of cake," said Snipp
as he started to climb up on the box.

The Gingerbread Boys Take Off

Snipp, Snapp, and Snurr climbed up
on the box.   Maybe Snipp was trying to see
too much.   Anyway, the box started to tip.
The three boys with the yellow hair fell
into the dark brown gingerbread batter.

The baker was so surprised that
his white cap fell off his head.
Then he fell down beside the batter.

As he sat there, just looking, Snipp,
then Snapp, then Snurr climbed out
of the gingerbread batter.

48

The boys were covered with the batter.
Their faces were covered with it. Even
their yellow hair was covered with it.

Their blue eyes looked like holes
in gingerbread faces.

Their clothes were covered
with the same dark brown batter.

They looked just like gingerbread boys.

"Let's hurry out of the bakery
before the baker catches us," said Snipp.
"He will be angry because we fell
into his batter."

All three ran headlong out of the bakery.
Mrs. Bunch happened to be near the door.
She was carrying a big bag of oranges
and a big bag of red apples.

The boys ran right into kind Mrs. Bunch.
Down she fell. Down fell the oranges
and the apples. Oranges and apples
covered the street.

Mrs. Bunch was so surprised to see boys
all covered with gingerbread batter
that she just sat on the ground
and looked at them. Oranges and apples
were all around her on the ground.

A big black cat had been sleeping
near the door of the bakery. The cat
saw the gingerbread boys too. Every hair
on the cat's back stood on end and
her eyes looked like balls of fire.

A dog that was near saw the boys.
The dog liked gingerbread better
than anything else. He started to run
after Snipp, Snapp, and Snurr.

A policeman saw the gingerbread boys
with the dog right behind them.

As he started after the dog,
the black cat got in his way. Down he fell
to the ground. The boys ran on
down the street with the dog nearer
to them than ever.

Just then four white horses trotted
down the street pulling a golden coach.

Riding in the golden coach was a princess.
The princess had seen the different things
that had happened. She was watching
the policeman when he fell over the cat.
She had seen Mrs. Bunch on the ground.

She had seen the dog as he started
after the gingerbread boys. She now saw
that the dog was getting nearer and nearer
to them. She thought they might get hurt.

The princess called to her coachman
to stop the coach. She told her footmen
to help the boys climb into the coach.

The golden coach stopped near the boys.

The two footmen didn't want three boys
covered with gingerbread batter to climb
into the clean coach. But the princess
was watching, so the footmen helped
the boys climb quickly into the coach.

Just as the dog came up to the coach,
the coachman quickly started the horses.
Away they went up a high hill.

The coach went faster and faster
over the ground. Soon the big dog
that liked gingerbread so well was left
far behind.

"Where are we going?" asked the boys.

"To the top of the hill," answered
the princess. "I live up there. I have
always wanted a gingerbread boy.
Now I have three right here with me.

We'll have a party with just the four
of us and my cat."

The golden coach stopped at the top
of the hill. The boys and the princess
jumped to the ground and went indoors.

"We'll use our golden dishes
for the party," said the pretty princess.
"Our baker baked cookies this morning.
We'll have some of those cookies.

There are big red apples on the trees
on the hill. You may have as many apples
as you can eat.

Best of all, we'll have ice cream
covered with toasted peanuts. There will
be big pieces of cake to go with it, too."

"It must be fine to live here and have
everything you want," said Snipp, Snapp,
and Snurr, their eyes almost popping.

The Princess Gives a Party

Soon the party was ready. The princess
looked very pretty as she sat at the head
of the table. She was wearing a white dress.
On her feet were pretty golden shoes.
By her side sat her white cat.

In front of the boys were golden dishes
full of ice cream, golden dishes full
of cookies, and golden dishes full of cake.

At the side of the table stood
three footmen. Each footman was ready
to give the boy near him more pieces
of cake, more cookies, and more ice cream.

The boys ate and ate and ate.

Never as long as they lived had they seen
so much to eat or a princess so pretty.

The boys ate all they wanted.

After they had finished eating,
the princess took them
to the flower garden. The white cat
walked by the side of the princess.

"Now I'll read you some fairy stories,"
said the pretty princess. There on top
of the hill the boys sat while the princess
read fairy stories to them.

Just as the princess finished reading
the stories, the four white horses
trotted up, pulling the golden coach.

The two footmen helped the boys climb
into the coach, but they were not happy
about it. Footmen don't like to have
gingerbread batter in a clean coach.

The pretty princess didn't like to see
the boys go. She asked them to come again
as soon as they could.

The footmen climbed up on the back
of the coach and it started down the hill
to the house where the boys lived.

For the second time that day, Snipp,
Snapp, and Snurr rode down the streets
of the town in the golden coach.

They did not see Mrs. Bunch.
She had put her oranges and apples back
into their bags and gone home.

But they did see the policeman. He put
his hand to his hat as they rode by.
By the side of the policeman sat the dog
and the black cat. The dog was so tired
he didn't even look up as they rode by.

58

The boys rode by the bakery. The baker
had placed some gingerbread men
in the window of the bakery. They had
yellow sugar hair, blue sugar eyes,
and pretty red sugar suits.

The gingerbread men looked just as
Snipp, Snapp, and Snurr had looked
when they went into the bakery.

The boys rode on to the house
where they lived. There the two footmen
helped them out of the golden coach.

Then the coachman called
to the white horses, and the coachman
and the footmen rode off.

Almost before Snipp, Snapp, and Snurr
had time to tell their mother
about the pretty princess and the party,
they were upstairs being cleaned up.

Their mother used hot water, and
the gingerbread came off very quickly.
The boys began to look very different.

Their hair was yellow again.
Their eyes were blue.

They put on their clean night clothes and
fell into bed. Their mother covered them.

As they started off to sleep,
Snipp began, "I — am — glad ——"

"I — am — not ——," went on Snapp.

"A gingerbread — boy," finished Snurr,
and they fell sound asleep.

In their sleep they saw again the hill
where the pretty princess lived
with her white cat. They rode up the hill
again in the golden coach.

This time the hill was made of ice cream
and gingerbread cookies. And all that
they found on top of the hill was
a big red apple.

The word **himself** is made by putting
the two words **him** and **self** together.

How is the word **herself** made?

What two words are put together to make
each of the following words?

myself   **yourself**   **itself**

One good way to help yourself learn
a new word is to look at the word itself
to see how it is made. What two words
make up each of these words?

anywhere downstairs outside whatever
inside   understand   doorway   daylight

What two parts make up each of these?

tonight   asleep   alike   without   forget

When do you really know a word?

When you use it to tell your thoughts
to others. When you can name it as soon
as you see it. When you read it
to yourself so as to make sense.

As you say the word **blue**, can you hear the sound that the letters **bl** stand for?

Say the words **blue** and **black** and hear the sound of **bl**.

Hear the sound of **sl** in **sleep**.

Hear the sound of **gr** in **green** and of **sn** in **snow**.

Take the **sn** from **snow**.

Put in **bl** to make **blow**.

Put in **gr** to make **grow**.

Put in **sl** to make **slow**.

Hear the beginning sounds as you say **snow, blow, grow, slow.**

Here are some questions to answer:

On what kind of days does snow blow?

On what kind of days do flowers grow?

Is it best to go a little slow when streets are covered with ice and snow?

The word **seen** is made by adding **n** to **see**.

To what word is the ending **n** added
to make each of the following words?

known   shown   thrown

"I might have known I'd hit a window,"
said Bob. "I should not have thrown
my ball at the house. I haven't shown
very good sense, I guess."

To make the word **eaten**, begin with **eat**
and put on the ending **en**.

How are these words made?

shorten   deepen

Do you shorten a string by cutting off
some of it or by adding some to it?

If you want to deepen a hole, do you dig
in it, throw things into it, or stretch it?

Before **en** is added to a word that ends
with silent **e**, the silent **e** is left off.

Taken is made by adding **en** to **tak**.

How are the words **given** and **whiten** made?

64

A Running Bird

Did you ever hear of a bird that could
run faster than a race horse?

Many birds can fly faster than horses
can run, but there is one bird that
can run faster than the fastest horse.
That bird is the ostrich.

Ostriches are strange birds. They have
wings, but they really can't fly at all.

Ostriches run along the ground. At times
they stretch their wings out as they run.
This makes them look as if they were
flying over the ground.

Sometimes on ostrich farms, the ostriches
run races with other animals.
The ostriches almost always win.

The Seven White Cats

No one ever believed in the seven white cats until he had seen them.

"Seven white cats! Silly! That can't be true!" That was what everyone said.

But there were the seven white cats, sure as could be. Anyone could see them if he took the trouble to walk up the hill to the farmhouse.

And there, too, was Katy Summers, who
lived on the farm with the seven white cats.

Katy had named them all.

The mother was called Blue Eyes.

The two big kittens were Pitter and Patter.

Pitter was a pretty kitten
with big blue eyes like her mother's.
Patter was funny looking, for his eyes
did not match. One eye was blue and
the other was yellow.

Then there were four little kittens.
They were full of fun and almost always
in trouble.

Katy had named three of them Snipp,
Snapp, and Snurr after the story children
that she liked to read about.

The fourth was called No-Tail. He was
always getting in the way. One day
he got under the foot of a farm horse.
After that he had only part of a tail.

Mr. Summers, Katy's daddy, did not like cats at all. He let Katy keep them only because she liked cats so much.

That is, he let her keep them until one day when nothing went right wherever the cats were.

When Mr. Summers went out to milk his cows, No-Tail ran along in front of him and got under his feet. Down fell Mr. Summers, milk pail and all. He was very angry with No-Tail.

Soon after that, Mrs. Summers found Blue Eyes helping herself to a big pan of cream.

That same day, Mrs. Summers found Snipp
asleep in the best bed upstairs.
She found Snapp playing
with the clean clothes on the line.
That was bad enough, but then
she found Snurr digging in the new garden.
That was just too much.

"Seven cats are too much trouble!"
said Mrs. Summers.

"There won't be any cats on this farm
after today," said Mr. Summers.

What Will Happen to the Cats?

Mr. Summers waited until Katy had gone to play with a little girl who lived near the farm. Then he put all seven cats into a big box.

He put the box of cats into the wagon and started off down the road.

First he rode up the hill to see Mrs. Bridge. Her little girl was glad to have a pretty white kitten. She wanted No-Tail because he looked so funny.

Then Mr. Summers rode down the hill.
He saw Mr. Lamb digging a new garden.

He said to Mr. Lamb, "Here is just
what you need. This cat knows just how
to dig up a garden."

With that, Mr. Summers put Snurr down
in Mr. Lamb's garden. Snurr liked that.
He began to dig right away.

Mr. Lamb was so surprised
that he couldn't say a word.
Mr. Summers rode on down the road.

Mr. Summers had only five cats left.
He looked at them and thought, "They are
pretty and Katy did like them very much.
Still, they were always in the way."

Then he came to Mrs. Field's house.

Mrs. Field had just put
her clean clothes on the line.

"Here's a cat that will help you
take down those clothes," said Mr. Summers.

He put Snapp down under the clothes line.
Before Mrs. Field could ask about the cat,
Mr. Summers was on his way again.
Now he had only four cats.

Down the road a little way Mr. Summers saw Mrs. Lock. She was carrying home a little pail of cream.

As he came near her, he said, "I have just the thing for you. Here is a cat that can help you with that cream."

It was hard to give Blue Eyes away. She had been around the farm a long time. But he was sure it should be done.

He handed Blue Eyes to Mrs. Lock. Now he had only three cats.

So Mrs. Lock took Blue Eyes home with her. It was no trouble because Blue Eyes was glad to go where cream went.

Soon Mr. Summers saw a mother
pulling her twin babies along
in a little wagon. Her little boy
was helping her.

"Your fine children should have
a pretty little kitten for their very own,"
called Mr. Summers.

The boy came over to look
at the three kittens left in the box.

"Choose a little one," said his mother.
"There isn't much milk left for a kitten
after three children drink all they need."

"Here's the only little kitten
I have left," said Mr. Summers.

He put Snipp into the boy's arms.

The boy looked at Snipp just the way
Mr. Summers had seen Katy look
at the kittens. Mr. Summers wasn't happy,
but he couldn't turn back now.

He tried to remember all the trouble
the kittens had been.

Down the street Mr. Strong had just
finished painting his house
a pretty light green. He stood looking
at it. It pleased him very much.

"Your fine green house will look
even better with a white kitten around,"
said Mr. Summers.

Before Mr. Strong knew
what had happened, he had Pitter,
the big kitten, in his hands.

Mr. Strong was surprised because he had
always thought that he didn't like cats.

Mr. Summers now had just one cat left.
He was beginning to wish that he had
never left the farm.

But Mr. Summers kept going.
Soon he came to a little house.
It was so near the side of the road that
he could look right in the windows.

By an open window sat old Mrs. Penny
who lived there all alone. She liked
to be at the open window where
she could watch people going by.

Mr. Summers walked up to the window
and put Patter into old Mrs. Penny's arms.

"There! You'll never be alone again!
Patter will look after you," he said.

Then he ran back to the wagon
before Mrs. Penny could say a word.

Now all the seven white cats were gone.
Mr. Summers started back to the farm.

Soon he began to think what Katy
would do when she found out that
her seven white cats were gone.

When he got home, he found Katy
in tears. She would not talk to him.
She would not eat anything.
She just sat and cried.
That night she cried herself to sleep.

There were still tears in her eyes
the next morning.

"This is more than I can stand,"
said Mr. Summers. "We must do something
to make her forget those cats."

"Why did you ever give them away?"
asked Mrs. Summers.

"I don't know why I ever did," he said.

Will Katy Forget?

That morning Mr. Summers said, "Katy,
I am going to the lighthouse today.
Would you like to come along?"

Katy had always wanted to go
to the lighthouse, but this morning
she didn't even smile. All she said was,
"All right, Daddy."

All the way to the lighthouse
Katy sat without saying a word.

All the way to the lighthouse
Mr. Summers thought of the cats.
He wished he had kept one of them
for Katy to play with.

As they came to the lighthouse,
they saw three kittens playing in front
of the door. One was black, one was
black and white, and one was all white
with blue eyes.

Katy ran over and took the white kitten
into her arms. Soon she began
to look happy.

"My white kitten likes you,"
said the man at the lighthouse to Katy.

Katy just smiled.

"Would you like to have that
white kitten, little girl?" he asked.

"Yes, I would," answered Katy.
"May I please have him, Daddy?"

"I guess so," said Mr. Summers.
"One cat should not be too much trouble."

Katy would not let the white kitten go,
even for a little while.   She didn't care
at all about going up the little stairs
to the light at the top of the lighthouse.

All Katy wanted was to go right home
with her little white kitten.

She was afraid that the man
might want his kitten back.

After a long time, Mr. Summers said,
"I guess we had better start home now."

Katy was ready and waiting in the wagon.

All the way home, Katy kept thinking
of what good times she would have
with a kitten. Having only one kitten
wasn't like having seven, but it was
much better than having none.

As they came to the gate of their farm,
Katy was almost happy. Then she
remembered. Always before when she had
jumped out of the wagon and opened the gate
all seven white cats had come running to her.

Now it was different! As she opened
the gate, not a cat did she see.

Then she heard a little meow.
She looked up and there coming around
the house was Blue Eyes. Along with her
were Pitter, Patter, Snipp, Snapp, Snurr,
and funny little No-Tail.

"Daddy! All my cats are back!"
cried Katy. "Please may I keep them all?"

Mr. Summers was so surprised to see
the seven white cats that all he could say
was, "I give up."

For some days people all over town were saying to each other, "Have you seen a white cat anywhere? Mine has run away."

If Katy ever heard about this, she didn't say a thing. She just smiled and kept on trying to hold all the cats in her arms at once.

Think Again

Said Andy Long to Tommy Green,
"Tonight I wish that I
Could be a very little boy
No bigger than a fly.

When Mother sent me up to bed,
I would not have to go.
I'd hide behind the cooky jar
And she would never know.

I'd find a fly with good strong wings
To ride up in the air.
And then I'd make a landing field
Right in my daddy's hair."

Said Tommy Green to Andy Long,
"Your daddy hits at flies.
So if you really care for fun,
It's best to stay your size."

Golden Days

The Hurdy-Gurdy Man

It was a fine spring morning in the town
of Indian Hills. Trees were beginning
to turn green. People were doing
their spring house cleaning.

A hurdy-gurdy man walked along,
looking for a place to get breakfast.
He was hungry, but he still whistled
happily as he looked around the town.

Soon the ragged hurdy-gurdy man came
to a store that was open.

The woman who owned the store was out
in front of it cleaning the windows.

"Good morning! May I get breakfast
in your store, my good woman?"
asked the hurdy-gurdy man. "I have
walked a long way this spring morning,
and I am very hungry."

The woman looked him over from head
to foot. His clothes were ragged, but
still he might have money to buy things.

The woman was about to say, "Yes,"
very politely. Then she saw
a funny little monkey looking at her
from behind the ragged hurdy-gurdy man.

The monkey didn't make a sound.
He just looked at the woman
with his two black eyes.

"I will sell you something, but you
can't eat or drink anything in my store,"
said the woman. "I can't stand monkeys!"

"Well, thank you!" said the man,
very politely. "I'm sure someone else
will sell us what we want." He walked away
whistling. On this fine spring morning
he just had to whistle.

The hurdy-gurdy man had not gone far
when he came to a bakery. There was
the baker in his white apron, putting
newly baked bread out on the counter
in his store. It smelled very good.

"Good morning," said the ragged man.
"How good your bread smells!
Will you sell us some of it and sell us
something hot to drink for breakfast?"

When the baker saw the monkey, he
wasn't as polite as the woman had been.

"I will sell you some bread to take
with you," he said, "but I won't sell you
anything hot to drink. I can't have
that monkey and you eating and drinking
in my store."

"Then I won't take the bread,"
said the hurdy-gurdy man politely.
"We'll find something to eat and drink
somewhere else, thank you."

Breakfast at Miss Gay's

On he walked that fine spring morning
and left the good-smelling bread behind.

Now it so happened that
the hurdy-gurdy man had come to a town
where everything was neat and tidy.
The houses were neat and tidy and
so were the streets.

All the people in the town worked
so hard keeping things neat and tidy
that they had no time for play.

The ragged and hungry man gave up
trying to get something to eat. He left
the stores and the neat and tidy houses
and walked in a pretty green park.

Near one end of the park he saw
two little houses side by side. They were
not neat and tidy. They needed painting.

They were not the kind of houses that
the people of Indian Hills liked to have
in their neat and tidy town.

Still, there was something gay
about the two houses. The strange man
saw that at once.

The ragged hurdy-gurdy man left the park
to get a better look at the two houses.
As he came near them, he saw that
there were signs in front of them.

On one sign he read:

Miss Gay
Dressmaking

The other sign said:

Mrs. Parks
Cleaning

From Miss Gay's house came the smell
of new bread. The hurdy-gurdy man went
through the gate and up to the side door.

Miss Gay was looking through the window.
She saw him and the monkey coming
up the walk. She opened the door and
came out to see the monkey.

"What a funny little monkey!" she said.

At that, the monkey jumped down
and ran through the doorway right
into Miss Gay's kitchen. He jumped
into a chair beside the table where
Miss Gay had been eating her breakfast.

"See that!" cried Miss Gay. "He must be
hungry. Maybe you are hungry, too.
Would you like some of my fresh bread
and something hot to drink?"

"I would, thank you," said the man
politely. "We have had no breakfast."
He followed Miss Gay through the doorway.

The kitchen was full of the smell
of fresh bread and fresh apple cake.

Miss Gay put two more chairs at the table.

94

"Sit down in these chairs while I get you something to eat and drink," she said.

She took from the oven the fresh bread and the freshly baked apple cake that smelled so good. She put them on the table and got a hot drink for the ragged man. She gave the monkey an apple to eat.

Then she thought of something. "I must call Tommy Parks who lives next door," she said. "He likes monkeys too."

She hurried out of the house calling, "Tommy Parks! Come and see who is sitting right here in my kitchen!"

Tommy came running through the doorway. How surprised he was to see a monkey!

The monkey liked Tommy right away and
wanted to give Tommy pieces of his apple.

As the hurdy-gurdy man ate breakfast,
he asked Miss Gay about the town.

"Many fine people live in Indian Hills,"
said Miss Gay. "They want to be polite
and kind, but they don't know how.

Where I came from, people would often
sit together and talk. Whenever there
was music, they came from far and near
to hear it. But here they are different.

They just sit in their chairs
in their neat and tidy houses. They never
have any fun when their work is through.

None of the people have learned how
to make any music. They won't even go
anywhere to hear music."

"They will come to hear my music,"
said the ragged hurdy-gurdy man.
"My music is as fresh as this spring air."

"Music is what they need," said Miss Gay.

Just then the queer little monkey
jumped onto the back of the chair on which
the hurdy-gurdy man was sitting.

"He thinks we should leave now,"
said the man. "I'll take him to the park.
We'll play some music there."

"And you must leave for school, Tommy,"
said Miss Gay.

"Thank you for the good breakfast,"
said the man politely. "I don't often eat
or even smell fresh bread like yours.
I don't often have a good hot drink
for breakfast."

"My school is right by the park,"
said Tommy. "I'll go with you."

Who Wants to Hear Music?

As they were leaving the house,
Tommy asked, "What music can you play?"

"I can play three different pieces,"
said the man. "But I don't often need
to play more than two.

If I pull out this first stop and
turn the handle round and round,
the first piece of music starts to play.
This second stop is for the second piece.
This third stop is for the third piece.
I do not often play that."

"Why not?" asked Tommy.

"It's a queer kind of music," the man said.

"I like queer music," said Tommy.
"I'd like to hear it before you leave."

When they came to the park near the school,
the man stopped. He took the hurdy-gurdy
off his back.

The hurdy-gurdy man pulled out
the first stop and began to turn
the handle. The first piece began to play.
It was merry music, not queer music
as the man had said the third piece was.

Round and round went the handle, and
on and on went the merry music.

No one came to hear the music at first.
However, by the time the merry music
was playing for the second time, many
of the children were there.

The children of Indian Hills were not
queer like the older people. They were
like the children of any other town.

The children made a ring
around the hurdy-gurdy man.
They knew that they should go to school,
but they couldn't leave the merry music.

Round and round went the handle
of the hurdy-gurdy. Bigger and bigger
became the ring of children.

By the time the second piece of music
began to play, all the school children
were standing in the ring.

Round and round went the handle
of the hurdy-gurdy. This piece was gayer,
faster, and merrier than the first.
The children began to dance in the ring.

The monkey pulled off his cap and danced too. This made the children laugh so hard that they almost fell over one another as they danced.

Then the teacher began to ring the school bell. Not one of the merry children dancing in the ring heard the bell.

After the bell had been ringing for some time, the teacher came out of the school. She called to the children, but not one of them heard her call.

The handle of the hurdy-gurdy still
went round and round. The children
danced on and on to the merry music.

Such a thing had never happened before
in Indian Hills. The teacher was angry.

Such things should not happen
on a school day. How could she teach
the children if they didn't come to school?

The mayor of the town could not think
what had happened. The school bell
had stopped ringing, but he had seen
no children leave the park for school.

The mayor wanted to call the policeman,
but the policeman was home in bed. He had
a bad cold in his head. It wasn't often
that a policeman was needed in the town.

So the mayor got out of the big chair
that the mayor always sits in and went
to tell the queer man to leave town.

"Go away with your hurdy-gurdy!"
called the mayor. "We can't have
such music in this town. Such music
is bad for children."

No one had heard the bell ring.
No one had heard the teacher call.
Now no one heard what the mayor said.

The handle of the hurdy-gurdy kept going
round and round. The children danced faster
and laughed more than before.

By this time the people of the town
were coming to see what was happening.
They were as angry as the teacher
and the mayor.

Just then, the monkey danced right up
to the mayor and climbed on his back.
He took the mayor's hat right off his head.
Then the monkey put the mayor's hat
on his own head and climbed up a high tree.

"Get that monkey! Lock him up!"
cried the mayor. "I can't have
such things happening here!"

The mayor was very angry, but
the handle kept turning round and round.

Then Tommy Parks came up
to the hurdy-gurdy man.

"Play the third piece! I want to hear
the third piece!" called Tommy.

The hurdy-gurdy man looked at Tommy.
He saw the ring of happy children.
He also saw the angry fathers, mothers,
and other people.

He stopped turning the handle
of the hurdy-gurdy.

"Yes!" he said. "I think this is
the right time to play the third piece."

Quickly he pulled out the third stop
on the side of the hurdy-gurdy. That was
the one that had made Tommy so curious.
Round and round went the handle again.

Out came the best, the merriest,
the gayest, and also the strangest music
that had ever been heard in Indian Hills
or in any other town.

The people forgot the monkey and also
the mayor's hat. Such surprised looks
had never been seen on faces before.

People started to wag their heads
in time to the music. Their feet began
to hop in the strangest kind of dance.

Before they knew it, they were dancing
as if they did such a thing every day.

Fathers and mothers danced as well
as the children. Miss Gay and also
Mrs. Parks danced with the mayor.

The policeman had climbed out of bed
to see what was happening in Indian Hills.
He was dancing with the woman who
would not have the monkey in her store.

The baker was dancing also. He was dancing with the schoolteacher.

The people were dancing as if they didn't have a care at all. They looked like the gayest, merriest people that ever were.

"Stop that music!" cried the mayor as he danced round and round.

Then the teacher also called, "Please, stop that music!"

"Stop it, please!" cried the mothers and fathers. "Such dancing is bad!"

But no one could stop the music!

The monkey came down from the tree
and sat on the hurdy-gurdy man's back.

Then all at once the music did stop!
Down fell every dancer, one on top
of another. The store woman fell
over the policeman. Mrs. Parks found
herself sitting on the mayor's feet.

There they sat looking at each other,
very red-faced.

How silly they all looked!

There was only one thing to do about it.
Everyone began to laugh. They laughed and
laughed until their sides hurt.

The mayor was the first one who could stop laughing long enough to talk.

"Let's have a picnic!" he said.

"Yes! A picnic! A picnic!" cried the children. "And let's have sandwiches and ice cream and cake."

"I'll bring fresh bread for sandwiches," said the baker as he sat up.

The store woman got to her feet. "I'll bring things to put into the sandwiches," she said.

"Let the fathers make the sandwiches," a man said.

"That takes care of the sandwiches," said the teacher. "I'll make lemonade. We can't have a picnic without lemonade."

"We'll make ice cream and cake for all who come to the picnic," said the mothers.

"And I'll bring apples and oranges enough for everybody in town," said the judge.

"Hurry up and get things done,"
the mayor said. "When everything is ready,
the fireman will ring a bell. Be sure
to wear old clothes to the picnic."

Everyone worked fast. The sandwiches
and cakes were put into boxes.
The lemonade was put into jars, and
the apples and oranges were put into bags.

It was to be the first picnic the town
had ever had. The spring day was just right
for it. The trees were green, the flowers
were pretty, and the air smelled as fresh
as the new bread in the sandwiches.

Soon the fire bell began to ring.
At the very first sound of the bell,
people came on the run from all over town.

All were dressed in old clothes, and
each one was carrying something to help
make the picnic a merry, merry time.

What a fine picnic it was! No one
kept count of how many sandwiches he ate
or how many glasses of lemonade he drank.

Never before had the children seen
more sandwiches, ice cream, cake, oranges,
and apples than they could eat.

The people were having so much fun that
they forgot about the hurdy-gurdy man.

Then all at once, Tommy Parks said,
"Where's the hurdy-gurdy man?"

Everyone looked around.
The hurdy-gurdy man was nowhere to be seen.

But you can be sure that, by this time,
the queer ragged man was walking and
whistling down some road, looking
for another little town that needed his music.

Room Enough

Many years ago a wise old judge lived in a little town.

Often people went to the judge for help with their troubles. It seemed to them that the wise judge could always tell them what to do.

One day an old man who lived
in a small house just outside the town
came to see the judge.

"I've heard that you are very wise,"
he said to the judge. "I hope that
you can help me."

"I'll help you if I can," said the judge.
"Tell me what seems to be the trouble."

"My wife and I have been living
all alone," said the old man. "Our house
is very small, but we have been happy
together. Some time ago my son and
his wife and baby came to live with us.

The house is now so full I can hardly
walk around in it. And the baby seems
to be always in my way."

"Doesn't your son help with the work
on your small farm?" asked the judge.

"Yes, he does," said the old man.
"He does almost all the farm work. But
the house is too small for the five of us.
If I had money enough, I would build
a bigger house."

"Doesn't your son's wife do anything
to help?" asked the judge.

"She is a good worker," said the old man.
"She takes care of the baby and helps
with the work around the house and farm.

If I could only build a bigger house,
I would be happy to have them with us.
But the one room in our house just doesn't
seem to be big enough for all of us."

"Does your wife like to have five people in such a small house?" asked the judge. "Does she want to build a bigger house?"

"The house doesn't seem too small to her," answered the old man. "She likes having our son and his wife and baby with us."

"I see," said the judge. "You want a larger house, but you don't have money enough to build one. Maybe I can help you. Will you promise to do everything that I tell you to do?"

"I'll promise," said the old man.
"I really need a larger house.
Everybody gets in my way now."

Then the wise judge said, "When you
get home, go into the barn and
get your cow and calf. Take them
to live with you in your small house."

"But will that make my house grow
larger?" asked the old man. "That seems
silly to me. It doesn't make sense."

"Did you come here for help?"
asked the judge.

"Yes, I did, and I promised to do
what you asked," said the old man.

"I will take the cow and calf
into our small house. I hope that this
will make the house grow larger.
It doesn't have room enough for me now."

When the old man got home, he went
right to the barn to get the cow and calf.

As he pulled them into the house,
his wife said, "What are you doing
with the cow and calf? Put them out
in the barn where they belong! They are
getting my clean floor all dirty!"

The old man told what the judge had said.

"If the judge said that taking the cow
and calf into the house would make it grow,
I believe it," said the old wife.
"The judge is a very wise man.

We haven't enough money to build
a new house anyway. If a dirty floor
will help us to have a larger house,
I'll put up with it."

A Cow and a Calf in the House?

Now things really did seem bad
to the old man. The floor was always
dirty. The little house was no longer
neat and tidy.

Every time the cow turned her head,
the bell on her neck would ring. The calf
often knocked things off the table.

No longer could the old man sit
by himself while the others worked. He had
to watch the cow and calf all the time
to be sure they didn't get into trouble.

Sometimes the calf nearly walked
on the baby as the baby played on the floor.
Then the poor baby would cry.

One day the old man found the cow
eating his food. He gave the poor cow
a big push and she knocked the dishes and
food off the table onto the dirty floor.

That was too much for the old man.
"I can't have this cow putting her nose
into my food," he said. "The house
doesn't seem to be growing any larger.
It seems to be growing smaller.

I'm going to see the judge again.
That cow has her nose in everything.
She puts her nose into my face at night
when I'm in bed. I can't even sleep."

The old man started for town to see
the judge.

The old man told the judge how the cow put her nose into everything. He told how the cow ate his food and knocked the dishes off the table onto the dirty floor.

Then he said, "I've kept my promise, but the house hasn't grown at all."

The wise judge heard everything. "It's too soon for the house to grow," he said. "Hasn't your poor wife said anything about the cow?"

"She hasn't said much," the old man answered. "She works so hard that she likes to have the cow in the house. Now she doesn't have to go to the barn to milk.

But that cow is more trouble to me than my son, his wife, and their baby. I can't sit still with her in the house, and she doesn't let me sleep at night."

"If you will keep your promise
a little longer, you will see that I am
right," said the judge. "Do as I say and
you will not have to build a bigger house.

Go home now and take the sheep
from the barn. Take the sheep
into the house to live with you."

"But if the house hasn't grown
with the cow and the calf, how can a sheep
make it grow?" asked the unhappy old man.

"Just do as I say and everything will be
all right," said the judge.

The old man said to the judge,
"A promise is a promise." To himself
he said, "If I were not so poor, I would build
a larger house." Then he started home.

And a Sheep, a Goat, and Pigs?

Soon the unhappy old man was home again.
He went to the barn and got the sheep.

His wife saw him coming with the sheep.
"What! Are you going to bring the sheep in,
too?" she asked.

"The judge said to do it,"
answered the old man. "He said that
it would make our house grow larger."

"The judge must be right,"
said the old wife. "He is a very wise man."

Before night the sheep had jumped
on the old man's chair and broken it.
The cow had broken a jar with her tail.
The calf had broken a pretty dish.

When the old man told his wife how
unhappy he was, she said, "Be patient
a little longer. I'm sure the judge is right."

The old man found it hard to be patient.

The next day the sheep jumped up on the old man's bed. Down went the bed to the floor, all broken!

That same day the cow put her nose into the cream that the old woman was making into butter. The cream had to be used to feed the pigs, and there was no butter to eat.

When the old woman was feeding the baby, the sheep knocked the dish of food right out of her hands onto the dirty floor.

"This can't go on," said the old man, looking at the pieces of the broken dish. "I am going to talk to the judge again."

The judge came to the door when
the old man knocked. "What now?" he asked.

The old man said, "My house hasn't grown
at all! The sheep has broken my chair and
my bed. Nearly all the dishes are broken.

My wife can't make butter because the cow
keeps putting her nose into the cream.
We have to feed the good cream to the pigs."

"Build a new chair and a new bed,"
said the judge. "Buy some new dishes.
Help your wife make more butter.

Now, when you go home, you must do
one last thing. Take the goat and the pigs
into the house to live with you."

The old man was very unhappy.
He knew that the pigs and the goat would
really fill the small house.

At last he said, "If you think this will
give me a larger house without building
a new one, I'll be patient and do it.
A promise is a promise."

As the old man walked slowly home,
he thought of this last thing he had to do.
"I hope that the house won't be so filled
with animals that the people will have
to sleep in the barn," he thought.

He walked more and more slowly as
he came nearer home. He was tired of living
in the dirty house with the animals.
It was hard for him to be patient.

When he came to the house, he found
his wife making butter. The cow was trying
to get her nose into the cream again.

His son's wife was trying to feed
the baby. The sheep was trying to get
the poor baby's food. The house seemed
filled with people and animals.

"What did the judge say?"
asked the old woman.

"He told me to bring the goat and
the pigs into the house," said the old man
slowly. "It doesn't make sense to me."

"Well, if he said that, do it and get it over with," said the old woman. "The judge is a wise man. This time I am sure that our house will get larger. We can be patient a little while longer."

So the old man went slowly to the barn. Soon he was back with the goat and the pigs.

The goat didn't want to go into the house, but at last the old man got him in.

The pigs were glad to get in. They began to look around for some food.

The house was so filled now that the old man could find no place to rest.

Did the House Really Get Bigger?

That day the goat pushed the old woman right into the cream that she was making into butter. A pig put his dirty nose into the poor baby's food. More dishes were knocked onto the floor and broken.

The old woman became very angry.

She said, "This can not go on. You must return to the judge. We can't be patient any longer. We can't work if we can't rest.

The baby is sure to get hurt in a house filled with animals. This morning he cut himself on a piece of a broken dish."

So the old man returned to the judge's house and knocked on the door.

When the judge saw the old man, he said,
"Well, why have you returned? Hasn't
your house grown large enough for you?"

"No, it hasn't," said the old man.
"You must help us. My poor wife can
no longer put up with the animals.
I am afraid they will hurt the baby.
The poor baby cuts himself on broken dishes.

My son and his wife can't get any rest
while the house is filled with animals.
They have been patient, but our house
hasn't grown any larger."

The judge smiled. "So at last you say it's
your poor wife who can't stand the animals.
And it's your son's wife and baby that
you are thinking of. At last you are
thinking of somebody else, not just yourself.

Well, go home and return all the animals
to the barn. Help your wife clean up
the dirty house. See what will happen."

The old man hurried home to his wife. When he came to the house, his wife was trying to make butter.

"At last the judge says to return all the animals to the barn!" cried the old man. "Help me get them out."

The old man and his wife pushed and pulled at the animals until not one was left in the house. The animals seemed glad to get back where they belonged.

Then the old man and his wife started
to clean the dirty house. They washed
the floor. Then they washed all the windows.
The old woman even washed the bed clothes.

Now the house began to look
neat and tidy again. It seemed
as if some magic were at work.

The old wife finished making the butter.
Then she washed the new dishes and all
the old ones that had not been
knocked onto the floor and broken.

The son's wife made a fine dinner
for the five of them, with food enough
to feed twice as many. No one was unhappy.
It all seemed like magic.

At last all the work was done.
The dishes were washed, the house was
clean, and the baby was sleeping soundly.

The patient old man and his wife and
the son and his wife sat down to rest.

"Hasn't this house grown!"
said the old woman. "The judge was right.
You kept your promise and the house really
has grown larger. It seems like magic.
We don't need to build a new house.

When you see the wise judge, thank him.
Tell him that we are glad that we waited
patiently for the house to grow."

Never again were the old man and
his good wife unhappy.

Oswald Makes Magic

Oswald Read prized two things
very highly. One was Agnes, his wife.
The other was his magic.

Agnes prized Oswald highly, too, but
sometimes she found it hard to live
with his magic. Things in her house
didn't stay where they belonged.
Oswald was always surprising her.

One day when Oswald came home, Agnes was looking troubled.

"My ring is gone," she said. "It isn't where I put it. Have you seen it?"

Oswald didn't answer her question.

"The flowers need water," he said. "I'll get a hose and turn on the water. Then I'll help find the ring."

Soon Oswald had the water running.

"Agnes, you hold the hose and I'll get my magic wand," he said.

Agnes took the hose and Oswald went into the house. After a while he came back with the magic wand in his hand.

"I looked everywhere in there," he said. "Now I'll take a look around here."

"I haven't had the ring out here," said Agnes as Oswald took the hose from her and turned off the water.

"I'll look around anyway," he said.

Oswald let all the water run out
of the hose. Then he took the hose in
his right hand and tapped it with his
magic wand.

Oswald waved the wand above the hose.
Then he waved the wand under it.
He turned the hose over and once more
waved the magic wand over it. Then he
put one end of the hose up to his eye.

"Just as I thought!" he cried.
"See, Agnes?"

He looked very wise, tapped the hose
with his magic wand, and out came the ring.

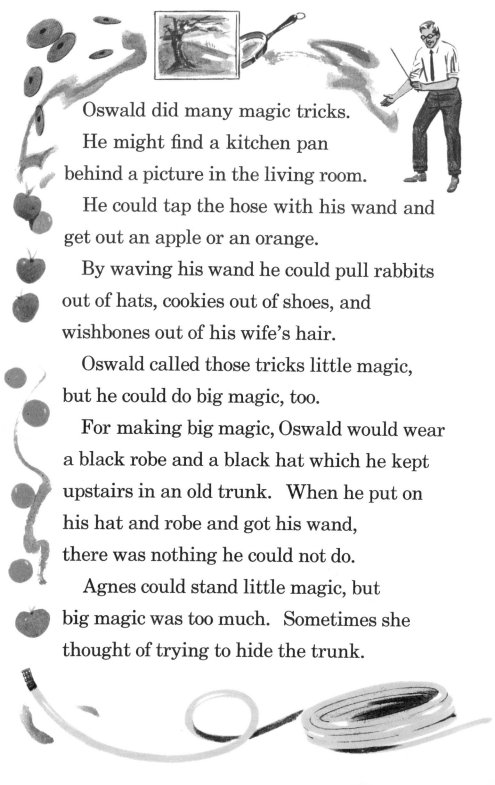

Oswald did many magic tricks.

He might find a kitchen pan behind a picture in the living room.

He could tap the hose with his wand and get out an apple or an orange.

By waving his wand he could pull rabbits out of hats, cookies out of shoes, and wishbones out of his wife's hair.

Oswald called those tricks little magic, but he could do big magic, too.

For making big magic, Oswald would wear a black robe and a black hat which he kept upstairs in an old trunk. When he put on his hat and robe and got his wand, there was nothing he could not do.

Agnes could stand little magic, but big magic was too much. Sometimes she thought of trying to hide the trunk.

One summer Oswald and Agnes had to find
a new home. He had no time for magic.
The hat and robe stayed in the old trunk.

Agnes didn't mind that, but Oswald did.

"Just wait!" he often said. "When we
get into our new home, I'll make the best
and biggest magic you ever saw."

Agnes made up her mind to hide the trunk.
She pushed it behind a door. She hoped
that Oswald could not make big magic
without his wand, robe, and black hat.

When the truck came to take things
to the new home, Agnes watched every piece
that went into it. The trunk was not put
on the truck. She couldn't help smiling
about the trick she had played on Oswald.

As the truck slowly started off, Oswald
jumped into it. Agnes got into their car.
As she went on ahead, she waved to Oswald.
He waved back and smiled.

At their new home Agnes went upstairs
to show the men where to put things.
Oswald helped them and the work went fast.
Soon he called, "Last piece coming up!"

There was Oswald with the trunk.
"I hope you don't mind," he said, smiling.

Agnes couldn't help laughing.
There was no way to stop Oswald's magic.

Behind the new home there was a garden.
Around that there was a fence,
a high board fence painted gray.

Agnes didn't care for the gray fence,
but she liked the garden. She could be
happy, looking at the flowers, or just
sitting still and hearing the birds.

Agnes hoped that Oswald would make all
his magic in the house. She didn't mind
his doing tricks, if she didn't have to be
right with them.

Oswald Works Outside

Oswald could see that Agnes was not happy about the gray fence.

He began to think about what he could put into the garden. He wanted something to make her forget the gray board fence. He wanted something that no one else had ever thought of putting into a garden.

One day Oswald happened to remember that Agnes had lived in a Chinese city when she was a little girl. She would surely like something Chinese.

Then Oswald thought of his magic. By using big magic he could get anything he wished. Oswald smiled and began to whistle.

The next day, when Agnes came home
from a party, she went to Oswald's room
to tell him about the fun she had had.
He wasn't there. The trunk was open and
the robe and cap were gone.

Agnes hurried to a window and looked down
into the garden. There by the gray fence
stood Oswald, dressed in his hat and robe.
He was holding the hose with one hand
and waving his wand with the other.

Agnes could hardly believe what she saw.

Under the hose a Chinese dragon was
playing around in the water.

The Chinese dragon was about as big
as three big dogs. He was red all over,
all but his feet and back. They were golden.

Agnes hurried down to the garden. When
the Chinese dragon saw her, he stood up
and began to blow fire through his nose.

Agnes jumped back quickly.

"Don't be afraid!" Oswald called.
"He won't hurt you. A Chinese dragon
blows fire through his nose to show that
he likes you. I hope you don't mind."

Agnes was very angry.

"What — where — how?" she cried.
She was too angry to finish a question.

The Chinese dragon stopped blowing fire
through his nose. He knew that something
must be wrong.

Oswald smiled his biggest smile.

"Big magic did it," he said. "It wasn't
very hard to do. Anyone can make
a Chinese dragon — if he knows how."

"How?" cried Agnes, still angry.

"I can't — I won't tell," said Oswald.
"It isn't wrong to make magic, but it is
wrong to tell how it is done. Isn't he
a fine pet?"

"Pet!" cried Agnes. "I don't like him!"

Big tears came into the dragon's eyes. Then he sat down by the gray board fence and cried right out loud.

"Now see what you did!" said Oswald.

"What I did!" cried Agnes. "I didn't do anything wrong."

"You talked too loud," said Oswald. "See how frightened he is!"

"If you think he is frightened, what do you think I am?" asked Agnes.

"Well, come and pet him," said Oswald. "Show him that you like him."

"I won't!" said Agnes. "I don't like him. Put him back where he came from before he frightens everybody around here. A Chinese dragon is no good to anyone."

"That's wrong!" said Oswald. "Just wait! I'll show you what a Chinese dragon can do!"

The dragon cried louder than ever.

"Poor little thing!" said Oswald.
"It's wrong to frighten him. I'll pet him
behind the ears. Dragons like to be
petted behind their ears."

Very soon the dragon stopped crying, and
Oswald whispered something in his ear.
The dragon stood up on his hind legs.

Oswald put a large pan of water on the
dragon's nose. At once the dragon began
to blow fire through his nose and
the water soon got very hot.

"There!" said Oswald. "Now shall I have
our pet make some cocoa?"

"Not for me!" said Agnes as she turned
quickly and went into the house.

The Dragon Makes More Trouble

The Chinese dragon soon learned that Oswald was his friend. He also learned that Agnes was not his friend. That made him feel very bad.

The dragon learned tricks very quickly. When he wasn't frightened, he did everything Oswald wanted him to do.

He would run like a cat along the top of the gray board fence. He would stand on his head. He would jump up, turn over and over, and land on his hind feet.

When Oswald petted him behind the ears, he would stand on his hind feet and blow fire in a friendly way. But when his feelings were hurt and he became angry, he frightened everybody.

When the dragon did something wrong,
Oswald would tap his head very lightly
with the wand. That frightened him and
hurt his feelings a little, but it did not
make him angry. Oswald was his friend.

When a dragon's feelings are hurt,
he makes a queer little noise. It is like
a cry that wants to come out but can't.

But when a dragon is angry, he makes
loud noises that frighten everybody.

Oswald had always been careful not
to tap the Chinese dragon hard enough
to make him angry.

One morning Oswald got a pan of water and went down to the garden. He wanted to surprise Agnes by having the dragon help him get breakfast. He thought he might have oatmeal, cocoa, and toast.

Oswald waved his wand and the dragon stood up on his hind legs and began blowing fire through his nose. Oswald put the pan on the fire, and soon the water was hot. Then something happened.

The dragon began to jump around and the pan fell off his nose. Some hot water hit Oswald. He forgot to be careful.

"Stop it!" he shouted, and hit the dragon with his wand. It was not a light tap.

The dragon was frightened and angry. He made a noise such as no one had ever heard before. It was so loud that it went right through the houses and frightened everybody.

No one could sleep with such a noise going on.

People jumped out of bed,
pushed up windows, and shouted for help.
The noise got louder and louder.

Agnes called the police and soon
a policeman was knocking at her door.

She opened an upstairs window,
feeling very angry and very silly.

"What's wrong?" the policeman shouted.

"The dragon!" Agnes shouted back.

"The what?" shouted the policeman.

"The Chinese dragon!" shouted Agnes.
"Oswald made one with his magic. It's out
in the garden. Be careful."

The policeman knew about dragons and
magic. He couldn't be frightened
by one noisy Chinese dragon. The dragon
must have known that, for he stopped
the loud noise when he saw the policeman.

The policeman smiled in a friendly way
at Oswald and asked, "Well, where did you
dig up this thing?"

"I did some big magic," Oswald answered,
feeling a little silly. "Is that wrong?"

"Magic isn't wrong," said the policeman.
"But this dragon is too loud and too noisy.
Most people don't like loud noises.
Their ears can't stand them.

And here's another thing. The mayor
won't let you keep this animal here."

"He isn't an animal. He's a pet,"
said Oswald. "Most people keep pets."

"They are careful to keep them quiet,"
said the policeman.

What Became of the Dragon?

That night everything was quiet.
The dragon slept quietly in the garden,
and people slept quietly in their houses.
Most of the trouble seemed to be over.

Agnes was so glad that next day she
asked some friends to have dinner with her
at a Chinese eating place. It was run
by some Chinese friends of Oswald.

When Agnes and her friends got there,
they found the door locked. In the window
was a sign that read: NOT OPEN TODAY.

That was all. No one around there knew
why the place was not open or where the men
had gone. So Agnes took her friends
to another good place for dinner.

When Agnes got home, she soon found out
where the Chinese friends had gone.   There
in the garden they sat by the gray fence.
The dragon was standing on his hind legs,
blowing fire through his nose.

As Agnes walked into the garden,
all the Chinese friends got up and bowed.

"Our friends came to see our new pet!"
said Oswald.   The friends bowed politely.
Then each one bowed and said hello to Agnes.
She bowed and said hello to them.

After that they went on quietly watching
the dragon.   He was feeling happy.

"Our new pet slept so well last night
that now he wants to play," said Oswald.

As he said that, the dragon tried
to blow fire down Agnes's back.

Agnes got so angry she hit the dragon
right in the face and boxed his ears.

That made the dragon angry. He made
such a loud noise that even the Chinese
friends were frightened. They covered
their ears and started to leave.

They were so frightened they said hello
and not good-by and forgot to bow.

"Don't go!" shouted Oswald. "I need help."

The Chinese friends came back. One of them petted the dragon behind the ears until he stopped making the loud noise.

As soon as everything was quiet, Oswald whispered something to his friends. They bowed and smiled and started off.

As they left, they wanted to say good-by but they forgot and said hello.

Oswald smiled and said hello to them. Then he went into the house to see how Agnes was feeling. She was unhappy.

"I can't stand that noisy dragon!" she cried. "Take him away or I'll leave!"

"I'll take care of him," Oswald said. "He will never trouble you again."

That night Agnes slept well. The dragon must have slept, too, for everything was very, very quiet.

The next morning when Agnes looked out
into the garden, the dragon was not there.
She hurried downstairs to the living room
where she heard Oswald walking around.

As she walked through the doorway,
Oswald smiled and looked up at a new picture
over the fireplace. It was a red dragon,
a sleeping red dragon with golden feet.

Agnes didn't ask where it came from.
She knew. At last Oswald had put his magic
to good use.

Oswald never again let the dragon play
under the hose or walk on the gray fence.
He wanted Agnes and her friends to think
that the dragon just slept on and on.

Now and then the Chinese friends came
to see the dragon.   They always knocked
at the door, bowed, and said hello.
Then they came in and sat quietly watching
while the dragon slept.

Sometimes when Agnes was away, Oswald
would have the dragon sit in the fireplace
and blow fire through his nose.
That always made the Chinese friends happy.

Agnes was always happy to show the dragon to her friends.

"It's a fine piece of Chinese work," she would say. "Just see how real it looks! You know, sometimes I have a strange feeling that it opens one eye a little way when I come into the room."

"How silly!" said her friends.

Agnes wasn't so sure. She knew Oswald and his magic. She knew, too, that magic can make dragons do strange things.

When You Grow Up

"When you grow up," said Mr. Long,
  "What do you think you'll be?"
"I just don't know," said Andy Long.
  "It's hard to choose, you see.

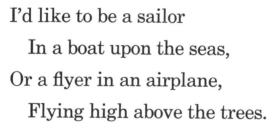

I'd like to be a fireman
  And go racing to the fires,
Or a linesman with his telephone,
  Working on the wires.

I'd like to be a sailor
  In a boat upon the seas,
Or a flyer in an airplane,
  Flying high above the trees.

I'd like to have a circus band
  And play in a parade,
Or work inside the circus tent
  Selling lemonade.

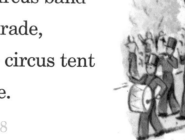

I'd like to run a tractor plow
   And push away the snow.
I'd like to be an officer
   Who lets the traffic go.

I'd like to be a mailman
   Or a keeper in a zoo;
And I'd like to be a banker,
   And have a railroad too.

I'd like to put in water pipes
   And sell things in a store.
I'd like to fish or ride a horse —
   All these and many more."

"When you grow up," said Mr. Long,
   "I hope you will not find
That you are out of work because
   You can't make up your mind!"

Sounds of Middle Letters

Say the word **at** slowly and listen
carefully to hear the beginning sound.
Did you hear the sound of the **a**?

It is not hard to hear the sound of **a**
at the beginning of a word.

Say the words **am, an, answer** slowly
and listen for the sound of **a**.

If you listen carefully, you can also
hear the sound of **a** when it comes
in the middle or near the middle of a word.

Say each of the following words slowly
and listen for the sound of the **a**
in the middle of the word:

back	**tap**	**black**	**glass**	**thank**
tack	**map**	**crack**	**class**	**crank**

If your class had to put up a map,
which of these things would be
of most help in the work?

good cracks   good cranks   good tacks

Listen to hear the sound of **e** that begins
the words **end, else, ever.** Say them slowly.

Now listen for the same sound of **e**
in the middle of each of these words:

let   get   when   sent   ten   them

As you say the following words,
make each middle **a** sound like **a** in **at,**
and each middle **e** sound like **e** in **end.**

sand   send   band   bend   man   men

pat   pet   than   then   bag   beg

Read each of the following questions
and choose the right answer for it:

Which of these things are hard to bend?

big boards   small wires   large bones

Which is the right way to pet a puppy?

Pat him.   Tap him.   Bend him.   Hit him.

What does the word **beg** mean?

Ask once.   Ask over and over.   Take.

Which is the polite way to get something
to eat at the dinner table?

Beg for it.   Ask for it.   Shout for it.

Say the words **in, into, is, if,** and **it,**
and listen to hear the sound of **i.**

Now listen for the same sound of **i**
in the middle of each of these words:

win   with   dish   string   think

As you say the following words, sound
each middle **a** like **a** in **at**, each middle **e**
like **e** in **end,** and each middle **i**
like **i** in **it**:

pan   pen   pin   sat   sit   bag   beg   big
fell   fill   tell   till   ten   tin   left   lift

Read each question that follows and
choose the right answer:

Which word means a place to keep pigs?

pan   pin   pen   tin   ten

If you want to buy some ice cream, which
of these things will help you most?

tin sense   ten sets   ten cents   tin cents

What is the best way to help a kitten
get out of a deep box?

Lift it out.   Throw it out.   Fill up the box.

The two letters **un** are sometimes used
before a word to add the meaning **not.**

Unhappy means **not happy.**

What does each of these words mean?

**unkind   unlike   untidy   unwise
unopened unlocked uncovered unseen**

Which looks better, a painted house
or an **unpainted** one?

If the ground is covered with snow,
how can it be **uncovered**?

Does the smell of spring flowers make
you feel **unhappy**?

In what ways is spring **unlike** summer?

In what ways is a sandwich **unlike**
a cooky?

If you need to **unlock** a door,
what do you have to use?

Is an **unlocked** door always open?

If you find an **unopened** letter that
is not yours, what should you do with it?

Money in My Bank

My bank is hungry all the time;
  I often have to feed it.
But there my money waits for me
  If I should really need it.

It eats up dollars, nickels, cents.
  As fast as I can earn them,
And there are times when I should like
  To have my bank return them.

Today I'd like to buy a game —
  I'm sure that I could use one —
A kitten or a puppy dog,
  It would be fun to choose one.

I wish I knew which one to buy;
  It's hard to choose between them.
I'll leave my money in the bank
  And just forget I've seen them.

164

Bob's Elephant

One day Bob Wise went to a circus. It was a large three-ring circus with every animal in it that anyone would ever look for in a circus.

In the ring right in front of Bob was the largest elephant that Bob had ever seen. Its ears were twice as large as the ears of any other elephant there.

That elephant was the largest animal that Bob had ever seen. He couldn't stop thinking about it. That night he slept very little.

The next morning he said, "Father, could I have an elephant for my birthday?"

"Maybe," answered his father. "But you'll have to wait until your birthday comes."

On the morning of his birthday, Bob asked for his elephant.

His father told him to open a large box that was in the living room. In it Bob found a large gray toy elephant. It was two feet high and it had to be pulled with a string.

Bob thanked his father politely
and played with the toy elephant
a little while. Then he put it away.

"Don't you like it?" asked his mother.

"Yes," answered Bob, "but I want
a real elephant with big ears,
like the one in the circus."

Bob's mother and father did not want him
to be unhappy. But they couldn't get
a real elephant for him.

Then his mother remembered that
there was a real elephant in the city zoo.

She thought, "The elephant in the zoo
belongs to all the people in this city.
It belongs to Bob just as much as
it does to anyone else."

"Bob!" she said. "Put on your hat.
I'm going to take you to see your elephant."

They rode for a while on the street car.
Then they got off and walked a little way.

Soon they were standing right in front
of a big cage. Inside the cage was
a large gray elephant, sound asleep.

"That's your elephant!" said Bob's mother.
"His name is Chief."

Bob was very happy. "Thank you, Mother,"
he said. "I guess I am the happiest boy
there is, because I have a mother like you
and an elephant like Chief."

Then he called to the elephant,
"Hello, Chief!"

Chief slept on.

"Poor old Chief," said Bob. "I guess
he's tired. Let's take him home."

"We can't do that," said Bob's mother.

"Why not?" asked Bob. "He's mine."

Bob's mother didn't want to tell him
that Chief belonged to all the people
in the city. She knew that Bob wanted
an elephant for his very own.

"Well, Bob," she said, "we have no place
to keep him. He's too big for any room
in our house."

"I guess he is," said Bob.
"He's too large for a house pet."

"And he eats so much! He would eat up
all of our food," said Bob's mother.

"That would be bad," said Bob.
"What can we do?"

"Why not leave him here?" said his mother.
"You may come back to see Chief tomorrow."

"All right," said Bob. "So long, Chief!"

Chief slept on quietly. The next morning Bob returned to Chief's cage. Chief was sleeping again.

"Hello, Chief!" Bob called loudly.

Chief slept on.

Just then a man came by carrying a broom.

"There's Chief's keeper, Mr. Bell," said Bob's mother.

"Hello, Mr. Bell," said Bob. "Why does Chief want to sleep all the time? What is wrong with him?"

"Nothing's wrong," said Mr. Bell. "He's just a bad elephant!"

170

Bob couldn't believe any elephant could
be bad. "He is my elephant," he said.
"My mother gave him to me for my birthday.
You take good care of him, don't you?"

Mr. Bell smiled. "I do my best, son."

"My name is Bob," said Bob.
"I don't think Chief is a bad elephant."

"He isn't good," said Mr. Bell.
"He just sits with his back to the people.
He sleeps most of the time. And he blows
water at me when he drinks."

"But elephants are fine animals,"
said Bob. "They can't be bad."

171

"Then tell me why Chief does bad things," said the keeper.

"I guess no one ever made him be good," said Bob.

"Are you going to teach him to be good?" asked the keeper.

"He's my elephant, so I'll have to," said Bob.

Every day Bob returned to the zoo to see Chief. He was very patient with Chief. Soon Chief knew him and liked him.

Bob would call, "Hello, Chief!"

172

Chief would make a big noise through his trunk. That was his way of saying, "Hello."

Then Bob would talk to Chief, saying, "Now look, Chief. You must be good. When you sit in your cage, face the people. You are not very pretty from the back."

At first Chief didn't seem to know what Bob was saying. Then one day he turned around. He sat that way every day from then on.

People began to stop to watch Chief.

"What a fine looking elephant!" they would say.

"His name is Chief," Bob would say. "He belongs to me!"

"Really?" the people would say. "He's a mighty fine elephant."

Then Bob would smile happily.

Chief no longer slept all day. Now he walked around, and sometimes he stood up on his hind legs. Once in a while he even seemed to smile and make a bow with his trunk.

Bob would talk to him or call to him, "Hello, there, Chief!"

Then Chief would make the big noise through his trunk.

"I'm surer than ever now that Chief
is a good elephant," Bob said one day.

"I'm not," said Mr. Bell. "He still
blows water all over me."

"Leave that to me," said Bob. "Bring me
the hose. I won't hurt Chief, but
I'll teach him not to blow water on you."

When Mr. Bell came with a pail of water,
Bob stood by. Chief took most of the water
into his trunk. Then he began to blow it
on poor Mr. Bell.

"Chief!" called Bob. "You stop that!"

But Chief wanted to play. He began
to blow water on Bob. The big elephant
seemed to be laughing.

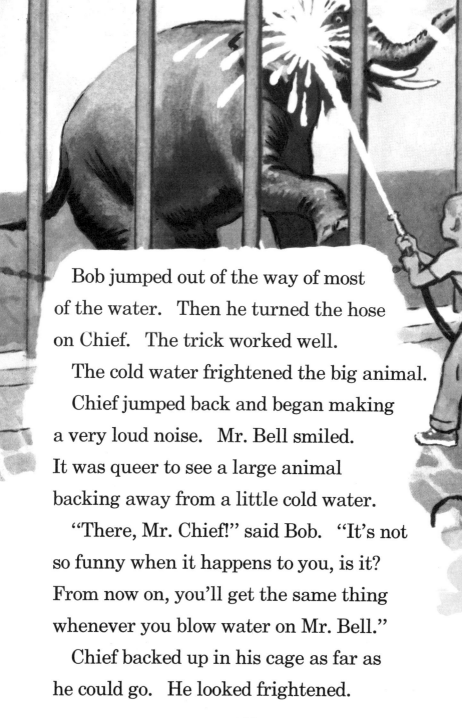

Bob jumped out of the way of most of the water. Then he turned the hose on Chief. The trick worked well.

The cold water frightened the big animal. Chief jumped back and began making a very loud noise. Mr. Bell smiled. It was queer to see a large animal backing away from a little cold water.

"There, Mr. Chief!" said Bob. "It's not so funny when it happens to you, is it? From now on, you'll get the same thing whenever you blow water on Mr. Bell."

Chief backed up in his cage as far as he could go. He looked frightened.

"Don't be frightened, Chief," said Bob. "We will not use the hose on you if you will promise not to blow water on Mr. Bell. Promise?"

It seemed to Bob that the big elephant wagged his trunk up and down as if he were promising to be good. Then he put the end of his trunk through the cage and took Bob's hand. They were friends again.

"Good boy!" said Bob. He put some peanuts into Chief's trunk.

Chief quickly put the peanuts into his mouth. Then he made the loud noise through his trunk. He was happy again.

All the Boys Own Chief

All summer long, Bob helped with Chief
until you could not have found
a better elephant.   Bob was pleased.
Mr. Bell, the keeper, was also pleased.
He let Bob feed Chief.

Then school time came again and Bob
returned to school with the other boys.

After school one day, the boys were all
telling what each one owned.

"I have a scooter," said Jack.

"That's nothing," said Andy.   "I have
a white dog.   It's the biggest dog
you ever saw."

"What of it?" said Bob.   "I own
an elephant!"

"That's silly!" said Freddy.
"Only zoos and circuses own elephants."

The other boys laughed at Bob.
They didn't believe him.

"All right!" said Bob.   "I'll show you."

Bob took the boys to Chief's cage.
Chief was sound asleep.

"There's my elephant!" said Bob.
"His name is Chief."

"He's not yours," said George.

"He is too!" said Bob.   "Hello, Chief!"
called Bob.

Chief jumped up, stood on his hind legs,
and made the loud noise through his trunk.

Bob gave Chief some peanuts.
Then Chief went back to sleep.

"There's nothing to that!" said Freddy.
"That old elephant will stand
on his hind legs for me, too."

Freddy called, "Hello, Chief!"

Chief did not even seem to hear.

"Chief!" called Freddy again.

Still Chief slept on.

"See!" said Bob. "He's my elephant
and he knows it!"

Now the boys were sure that Bob was right
and that he really owned Chief.

"Who gave him to you?" asked Andy.

"I got him on my birthday from Mother,"
said Bob.

The next day Bob's mother was called
to the school. The teacher told her
that all the boys were very unhappy
because they did not have anything
so fine as Bob's elephant.

"What shall I do?" asked Bob's mother.

"Tell Bob who really owns the elephant,
said the teacher.

So Bob's mother took Bob out of the room
to tell him who really owned Chief.
She told him that Chief really belonged
to all the people who lived in the city.

"Am I one of the people?" asked Bob.

"Yes," said Mrs.Wise.

"Then Chief really belongs to me,"
said Bob.

"Yes," said Mrs. Wise, "but he belongs
to the other boys, too. Tell them that."

"Why?" asked Bob.

"They are unhappy," said Mrs. Wise.
"They want an elephant too."

"Why can't they have one?" asked Bob.

"Chief is the only elephant in the city,"
said Mrs. Wise. "It would be fine if you
would make the other boys feel that
they own him too."

"Chief and I are friends," said Bob.
"We don't need anyone else."

Mrs. Wise let Bob think about it a while.

When the time came to go out to play,
none of the boys wanted to play.
They just sat and thought about owning
an elephant. They were very unhappy.

Nobody wanted to play with Bob.
He tried to play alone, but that was no fun.

That night Bob did not eat any dinner.

"What's wrong?" asked Mrs. Wise.

"It's no fun playing alone," said Bob. "The other boys won't play with me because of Chief."

"Maybe you should show them that you are their friend," said his mother.

Bob thought about it for a while.

"Mother, would it work if I told them they can own Chief too?" asked Bob.

His mother smiled and said, "You might try it and see if it works."

After school the next day, Bob took the boys to see Chief.

"Mother and the teacher say that
you want an elephant too," said Bob.

"Yes, we do," said Jack.

"Chief is the only elephant in the city,"
said Bob, "and I own him."

"We know that," said Andy.

"But I think you could all own him
with me," said Bob.

"He's big enough for all of us,"
said Freddy. "We are not very big boys."

"That's right," said Bob. "From now on
we all own Chief."

"Really?" asked George.

"Yes," said Bob. "You see, Chief
really belongs to the people of the city.
That's who we are. So we all own Chief."

"Does Chief know about it?" asked Andy.

"I'll tell him," said Bob.

He called, "Hello, Chief!"

Chief stood up on his hind legs and
made the loud noise through his trunk.

"Chief, I want you to hear this,"
said Bob. "These boys are your friends.
They own you as much as I do. We all
own you together. Do you understand?"

Chief made his trunk and head go up and
down as if he were saying, "I understand."

"All right," said Bob. "From now on,
when they call to you, answer them."

Then Bob turned to the boys. "Go on,
call him," said Bob.

All together the boys called,
"Hello, Chief!"

Chief looked at them. Then he got up
on his hind legs again and made
the big noise through his trunk.

Big smiles covered the boys' faces.

"What did I tell you?" said Bob.
"Now we all own an elephant."

Chief made the big noise
through his trunk once more.

"See?" said Bob. "Chief likes it, too."

Magic Times

The Story of a Clown

Once upon a time, all clowns lived on a small island far out in the sea. It was called Clown Island.

Clown Island was a very gay place because everyone there was always trying to be funny.

All the boys on Clown Island hoped
to become clowns.   So they went
to Clown School to learn the things
that clowns must do.

Every boy learned how to juggle things.
In Clown School you might see a boy
catching balls, pans, apples, or
anything else that he could throw
into the air.

The boys learned how to turn somersaults.
Some of the best clowns could turn
somersaults so fast that they looked
like balls turning round and round.

Every boy had to do more than learn
juggling and turning somersaults.
He had to think of tricks of his own.

Each boy who went to Clown School
got a report card to take home. It was not
like the report card you get. Report cards
from Clown School did not show
how well boys did in reading and numbers.

In Clown School a boy's report card
showed how good he was at juggling things
and turning somersaults. The report card
also showed how well he did in thinking up
tricks to make people laugh.

Every boy on Clown Island worked hard.
He knew that if he became a good clown,
he would get work in a good circus.
If he did not become a good clown,
he would have to stay on the island.

Learning to juggle five or six balls
was hard, and so was learning to turn
one somersault after another. But
the hardest thing of all was to think up
funny tricks that would make people laugh.

One of the boys who went to Clown School was named Eemi.

Eemi was a fine juggler. His report card always said, "Juggling — very good." There was no better juggler on Clown Island.

Eemi was good also at turning somersaults. His report card said, "Somersaults — very good." No one could turn somersaults faster than Eemi.

But Eemi was not good at thinking up tricks and jokes of his own. It made him feel bad to read on his report card, "Tricks and jokes — poor." It made his father and mother feel bad, too.

"I will try harder," Eemi promised.

Day after day Eemi juggled balls, pans, hats, caps, shoes, or anything else that he could throw into the air and catch.

Day after day he turned somersaults.

And day after day he tried to think up some funny tricks and jokes.

Every day his mother would ask, "Did you do well in school today, Eemi?"

Always Eemi would answer, "I did well in juggling and in turning somersaults."

"Did you think up any good jokes or tricks?" his father would ask.

"Not today," Eemi would say. "But I'll work harder so that I can pass the tests at the end of the year."

Eemi was sure he could pass the tests in juggling and in turning somersaults. But he was afraid of the test in thinking up tricks and jokes of his own.

And every clown had to pass that test.

The day before the tests were to be given,
a letter came to Clown School. It was
from the owner of the biggest circus
in the whole world. The letter said:

"I am looking for the best clown
in the whole world. There is a place
for him in my circus. Send him to me
when you find him."

That was just the place Eemi wanted.

He smiled as he thought of being a clown
in the biggest circus in the whole world.
People would watch him juggle things
and turn somersaults. How they would
laugh at his tricks and jokes!

All at once the smile left Eemi's face.

"What if I don't pass the test
in thinking up jokes and tricks of my own?"
he said to himself. "If I don't pass,
I'll have to stay here on Clown Island
and do work that is no fun at all."

194

The First Trick Goes Wrong

The tests were given in a long room. At one end of it sat ten judges, dressed in long black robes and black caps.

Every judge had a long gray beard. The chief judge had the longest beard of all.

Eemi knew that those ten judges were once the best clowns in the whole world. They had juggled and turned somersaults. They knew what it took to make a good joke or a good trick.

195

The tests began on Monday morning.

When Eemi's turn came, he walked quickly to the front of the room, bowed, and faced the ten judges. He could see that they had kindly faces behind their long beards.

He had no trouble in passing the tests in juggling and turning somersaults. But when he tried to think up a trick or a joke, his mind seemed to stand still. He couldn't think of anything at all.

The judges wanted Eemi to pass the test. They put their ten heads together and whispered through their ten gray beards. Then the judge with the longest beard called Eemi.

"We want you to pass this test, Eemi," he said. "This is Monday. You may have until Thursday. But you had better look around now for some useful work to choose if you don't pass the test on Thursday."

Eemi didn't like to think of staying
on the island, but he did as he was told.
On that very Monday he went to a bakery.

The baker was taking loaf after loaf
of good-smelling bread out of the oven.

"Do you bake bread every Monday?"
Eemi asked as the last loaf came out.

"Yes," said the baker. "Most people want
a loaf or two of fresh bread on Monday.
They want cream puffs, too. I'm going
to make cream puffs now. How about
helping me?"

"I'll be glad to help make cream puffs,"
said Eemi. "I could work until Thursday.
I try my test again on Thursday."

Eemi made cream puffs all the rest
of that Monday.   By night he had made
more cream puffs than he could count.

As he was taking the last pan of puffs
from the oven, the pan almost fell.

Eemi caught the puffs quickly, but they
were too hot to hold.   He began
to juggle them.   Then, one by one,
he put them onto the table.

The baker couldn't believe his eyes.
Not even one cream puff fell to the floor.

"A clever trick!" he cried.   "Very clever."

All at once Eemi had a happy thought.
"May I have ten cream puffs?" he asked.

"Twice ten," said the baker.   "And take
a loaf of fresh bread to your mother."

198

All the way home that Monday night Eemi thought how clever it would be to juggle cream puffs before the judges.

"I'll juggle puffs above their heads," he said to himself. "Their ten beards will stand out like ten brooms as they watch me. They will be sure to send me to the biggest circus in the whole world.

I won't wait until Thursday to try the test again. Tomorrow is Tuesday. Tuesday will be my lucky day."

Eemi hurried into the kitchen and gave the loaf of bread to his mother. But he took the bag of cream puffs up to his room. When he came down, he took some dishes and juggled them just for good luck.

"Son, you passed your tests, didn't you?" his mother cried.

"No, but I will tomorrow," said Eemi. "Monday didn't bring good luck, but I'll have good luck tomorrow. Tuesday will be my lucky day. I have thought up the cleverest trick in the whole world."

On Tuesday morning Eemi took the bag of cream puffs and went to the testing room. As he opened the door, he saw the line of black robes and gray beards at the other end of the room.

Eemi turned a somersault at the door and kept on turning somersaults until he was standing before the judges.

"Today is only Tuesday," Eemi said. "Do I have to wait until Thursday to show you the clever trick I thought up on Monday?"

"No," said the judge who had the longest beard. "Tuesday is as good as Thursday. Go ahead."

How glad Eemi was that he had stayed up late on Monday night to learn the trick! Soon he was juggling all the cream puffs high above the heads of the judges.

The judges were much pleased to see a young clown do such a clever trick. Smiles covered their faces. Their beards stood out like brooms as their eyes followed the flying puffs.

"I am the cleverest young clown in the whole world," thought Eemi. "Tuesday is surely my lucky day."

Eemi turned his head to look
at the judges. That was bad, but he
found it out too late. His left hand was
too late to catch a puff. His right hand
was too late. Then both were too late.

One after another, the cream puffs fell
into the faces and beards of the judges.

"Do you call this a clever joke?"
shouted the chief judge as he pulled
a cream puff out of his beard. "Even
a young clown should have better sense."

Eemi's good luck was gone. It was
too late to get it back. "Oh, dear! Oh, dear!
Oh, dear!" he cried as he ran out the door.

Will the New Trick Work?

Eemi ran and ran. At last he sat down
and put his head in his hands.

"Oh, dear! Oh, dear! Oh, dear!" he cried.
"This morning the whole world seemed gay.
Then my clever trick went all wrong.
Tuesday isn't my lucky day at all."

Some time later Eemi looked up and saw
a farmer working in a field.

"Farming is useful work," he thought.
"I guess I can learn to feed horses and
pigs and hens. I won't have to be clever
to do that. I'd better try it."

The farmer was glad to have help.
He had Eemi clean out the barn
and the hen house. Then he told Eemi
to feed the hens. Eemi liked that work.

The hens were so friendly they flew up
and sat on Eemi's arms. If he tried
to throw them off, they flew up and then
came right down and sat on his arms again.

Again and again Eemi watched the hens as
they flew up and came down on his arms.
Then he began to smile. He had thought up
a clever trick to try on Wednesday.

"Please, Mr. Farmer, may I have a bag?"
asked Eemi. Then he whispered something
into the farmer's ear.

"Surely!" said the farmer and smiled.

Late that night Eemi started home
with the bag. The farmer waved to him
and called, "Good luck to you, Eemi!"

"Thanks," said Eemi. "I'm sure that
Wednesday will be my lucky day."

Eemi was careful not to make any noise
as he went upstairs with the bag. He went
right to bed and slept well.

As daylight was coming on Wednesday,
Eemi's father and mother began to hear
strange sounds from Eemi's room overhead.
They heard the sounds of somersaults and
also something like the sound of wings.

Eemi was late to breakfast, but he
looked so happy, his mother didn't mind.

"Tuesday was your lucky day," she said.

"Tuesday was unlucky," said Eemi.
"But Wednesday will be lucky. I'll show
the judges what a clever young clown I am.
I have the best trick in the whole world."

Right after breakfast he got his bag and
started off. As he went out the front gate,
his mother and father waved to him
and called, "Good luck to you, Eemi!"

"Wednesday will be my lucky day,"
he called back.

The judges were surprised when Eemi opened the door that Wednesday morning. After his poor joke on Tuesday, they thought he might never come back to try tests again.

Other young clowns were taking tests, so Eemi waited at the door for his turn.

When it came, he opened the bag and out flew twelve hens. Then he stretched out his arms and six hens flew up and sat on each arm. All twelve sat very still.

"Ready!" he called. Up went his arms and up flew the twelve hens. As Eemi turned a somersault, the twelve hens turned somersaults, too. And as he landed on his feet, they landed on his arms.

All the way from the back to the front
of the room, Eemi and the twelve hens did
their clever trick. Now they were almost
in front of the judges. One more somersault
would be enough.

Up flew the twelve hens. As Eemi made
the last turn, he took a quick look
between his legs to see if the judges
looked pleased. Bad luck followed.

Eemi landed on his back and rolled
under the table. Before he could roll out,
the twelve hens came down. Eemi's arms
were not waiting for them. He was too late.

The twelve hens didn't know what to do.
They flew this way and that. Ten of them
flew into the beards of the judges. Maybe
the hens thought that the beards were nests.

Eemi looked out from under the table.
There the ten hens sat on the beards
of the judges, as if they were on nests. The
other two were sitting on the table.

The hens must have thought the beards were nests, and they knew what nests are for. In no time at all they laid ten eggs.

"Eemi! Eemi!" the chief judge shouted. "What kind of joke is this? These hens have laid eggs in our beards! Get them out before the eggs are broken."

Eemi rolled out from under the table, but he was too late. As the ten hens flew off the nests, they broke every egg that they had laid.

Eemi saw the broken eggs running down the judges' beards and robes. "Oh, dear! Oh, dear! Oh, dear!" he cried as he ran from the room. Wednesday, too, was unlucky.

Eemi ran home crying, "Oh, dear! Oh, dear! Oh, dear!" every step of the way. Wednesday had been even more unlucky than Tuesday.

Eemi's father went back and got the twelve hens so that Eemi could return them to the farmer as he had promised.

"Did you have good luck?" the farmer asked.

"No, I had bad luck," said Eemi. "I fell down and the twelve hens got frightened.

Ten flew into the beards of the judges and laid eggs there as they would in nests. The eggs broke and ran all over the judges' beards and robes.

The judges said that wasn't a clever joke. They said that a young clown should have more sense than to play bad jokes on them."

That Wednesday night Eemi's father said, "Thursday is the last day of the test, Son. If you don't pass the test, you must ask the judges to give you the paper that will show you what work you are to do."

Will Eemi Pass?

Eemi's bad luck on Tuesday and Wednesday
had made him too unhappy to try any tests
on Thursday. He made up his mind to go
to the judges, choose some useful work,
and ask for his working paper.

Eemi called his dog when he was ready
to start. He would feel better if he had
the little dog trotting along by his side.

"What shall I choose?" he asked himself
as he took the first step.

"Baker!" he said.

"Fireman," he said at the next step.

"Farmer," at the next step.

At each step he named some useful work.

He was saying, "Farmer," when he took
the step that left him standing
at the door of the testing room.

Eemi opened the door and stepped inside.

He saw all the boys who had taken tests.
Those who had passed had report cards
that said, "Passed." All the rest had
working papers. Each paper showed
the work that the boy was to do.

Eemi stood silent on the long carpet
that ran from the door to the judges' table.
The little dog waited quietly.

"What now, Eemi?" the chief judge asked.
"Do you want to try the test again?
If you do, don't try any jokes such as
you played on Tuesday and Wednesday."

Eemi was thinking hard just how to tell
the judges that he would choose farming and
how to ask for his working paper. He was
so frightened that when he opened his mouth
no sound came out.

"Come here, Eemi!" called the chief judge.

As Eemi took the first step, his foot
caught in the carpet. Down he fell.

He tried to get up, but again the carpet
caught his foot.   As he fell, he started
to roll.   One hand caught the carpet and
pulled it around him as he rolled over.

The little dog thought Eemi was playing.
It jumped on top of the carpet roll.

Over and over Eemi rolled, and always
the little dog stayed on top of the carpet.
The harder Eemi tried to stop, the faster
the carpet rolled on.

The rolling carpet hit the young clowns
and knocked them down like pins in a game
of tenpins.   Report cards flew all around.
On went the carpet until it hit the table
where the judges sat.

When the rolling carpet hit the table,
Eemi tried to get up, but he fell back
and started to roll to the door.
Faster and faster went the rolling carpet
with the little dog right on top of it.

It hit the line of boys who were holding
their working papers, and over they went
like the pins in a game of tenpins.
The papers flew into the air.

Through the door and into the street
the carpet rolled with the little dog
riding on top of it. Then across the street
it rolled and bounced until it was stopped
by a fence.

Poor Eemi! What an unhappy ending
for all his hopes! Everything had gone
wrong. Bad luck was following him.

On Monday he thought up a clever trick.

On Tuesday he covered the faces and beards
of the judges with cream puffs.

On Wednesday the hens laid eggs
in the beards of the judges.

Now, on Thursday, he wasn't trying to be
clever, but bad luck was still after him.

There was only one thing left to do.

Eemi pulled himself out of the roll
of carpet and went back to the judges
to ask for his working paper.

He was surprised to find them talking
and laughing. He was surprised, also,
when the chief judge smiled at him and
handed him a long roll of paper.

"Best wishes, Eemi!" said the chief judge.

Eemi took the paper and stood silent.

"My working paper," he thought.

"Read it," said the chief judge.

Eemi unrolled the paper.
Across the front of it in large letters
was the word PASSED.

"Your carpet trick surprised us, Eemi,"
said the chief judge. "Surely it is
the funniest trick in the whole world.
Tomorrow you will get on a boat and go
to the biggest circus in the whole world."

Eemi could hardly believe his eyes or
his ears, but at last he remembered to bow
politely and thank the judges.

215

The next morning all the people
on Clown Island were at the boat to see
Eemi off and to wish him good luck.
Even the judges in their black robes
were there.

Eemi went on board and stood where all
could see him. In his hand was the roll
of paper that said, "Passed."

At his side was the long roll
of red carpet, and on top of the roll sat
his little dog.

The boat began to pull away.

"Good-by, Eemi!" shouted everyone.

"Good luck!" called the farmer and
the baker.

Too Much Washing

Said little Billy Ball one day,
"When I'm no longer small,
I'll go somewhere that's far away
And never wash at all.

I wash my hands; I wash my feet,
My face, my arms, my hair.
Someday I'll wash myself away
Until I'm only air.

I think that Father's hair was washed
Too much when he was small,
For on his head, where hair should be,
There is no hair at all.

But Mother says this is not so —
That washing is not bad —
For look how well her hair has grown
From washings it has had."

The Queer Apron

Once upon a time there was
a Little Old Woman. She lived
in a little yellow house with a blue door
and two blue window boxes. Pretty flowers
were growing in both window boxes.

218

All around her neat and tidy house was
a blue fence.   Inside the fence was
the Little Old Woman's garden.   All kinds
of good things to eat were growing there.

It seemed as if anything
the Little Old Woman's fingers touched
was sure to grow.   People said that
her fingers were like magic in a garden.

The Little Old Woman could do more
than just grow things in her garden.
She could think.

She called this thinking "using her head."
She often said, "What is the good
of having a head if you don't use it?"

Whenever the Little Old Woman had
any trouble, she would use her head
to find out what to do.

She didn't think in the same way that
you or I would.   Not at all!   She had
a very different way of thinking.

This is the way she used her head to think:

First, she tied a wet rag around her head. Then she sat down, touched the tip of her first finger to her nose, and shut her eyes.

With one finger touching her nose and with her eyes shut, she would begin to think. She would think and think until she knew what to do.

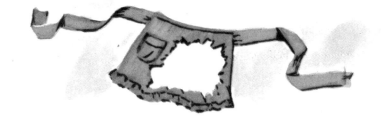

One morning the Little Old Woman started
to tie on her apron. There was a large hole
in the front of it. Once the hole had been
no bigger than the end of her finger.
Now there was more hole than apron.

It was plain to the old woman that she
needed a new apron. She could see that,
even with her eyes shut. But she had
no money to buy one. She was very poor.

"I could make an apron if I had
some money to buy cloth," she thought.
"Now is the time to use my head."

So she tied a wet rag around her head.
Then she touched the tip of her first finger
to her nose and shut her eyes. She sat and
thought and thought with her eyes shut
and her finger touching her nose.

Soon it was plain to her that
there was something that she could do.

"Why, it's all plain to me now," she said. "All I needed to do was use my head a little.

I will look in the bag where I keep my pieces of cloth. I may find a piece that is big enough for an apron."

The Little Old Woman got out the bag in which she kept her pieces of cloth.

The first piece that her fingers touched was blue. But it was no larger than an apron pocket.

"This blue cloth would make a fine pocket for an apron," she said. "But what good is an apron pocket without an apron?"

She laid it to one side and pulled out a piece of red cloth. It was a long piece, but it was only as wide as a necktie.

"This red cloth is just wide enough for a pair of apron strings," she said. "It is long enough to make a pair that will tie behind me."

"What good is a pair of apron strings
without an apron to sew them to?"
she asked. So she laid the narrow piece
of red cloth to one side.

Next she pulled out a piece of black cloth.

"I can plainly see that this black cloth
is wide enough," she said. "But it is
so long that it would touch the ground.
Who wants an apron to touch the ground?"

So she also laid aside the black cloth.
Then she took a purple piece from the bag.

"I should like a purple apron very much,"
she said. "This piece is not too wide and
not too narrow. But I can plainly see
that it is too short. I couldn't use
an apron as short as that."

So the Little Old Woman also laid
the purple cloth aside.

The Little Old Woman pulled out
other pieces, one by one.

Some were too wide, some were too narrow.
Some were too long, and some were too short.
Not one piece was just the right size
for an apron.

At last there was just one piece left.
It was yellow with green dots.

"I hope that I can use this piece
for my apron," said the Little Old Woman.
"It's not too wide, and it's not too narrow.
It's not too long, but it does seem
a little short.

However, if I cut and sew it carefully,
I think I can make a fine apron out of it."

So the Little Old Woman took her scissors
and cut out the apron very carefully.
She made it as large as she could
from the cloth that she had.

Then with her scissors she cut the pocket
from the blue cloth. Next, she took
the long, narrow piece of cloth. From it
she cut a pair of apron strings to sew
onto the apron.

She pinned them all together.
Then she tied the apron on to see
how it would look.

"It's wide enough, but it's
a little short," she said to herself.
"I need another piece of cloth just like
this one to make a ruffle to sew
onto the bottom. I like ruffles.

But where am I to get another piece
of yellow cloth with green dots in it
for a ruffle? The ruffle must match
the rest of the apron."

"I shall have to use my head," she said.
"Maybe I'll think of a way to get
some more cloth for a ruffle."

So she tied a wet rag around her head.
Then she touched her nose with the tip
of her first finger and shut her eyes.

She used her head and used her head.

Soon she knew where she could get
a ruffle to sew onto the bottom of the apron.

"First I'll cut a narrow piece
off the top of the apron with my scissors.
Then I'll make it into a ruffle and sew it
onto the bottom of the apron.
That will make the apron longer.

What a wise old woman I am!"

So she took her scissors and cut
a narrow piece off the top of the apron.
She made this narrow piece into a ruffle.
Then she sewed the ruffle onto the bottom
of the apron.

Next she sewed on the blue pocket.

She took the pair of narrow strings
that she had cut from the red cloth.
She sewed on the pair of strings so that
she could tie the apron on.

When the apron was all finished,
the Little Old Woman tried it on.
She stood before the looking glass as she
tied the apron strings.

"Dear me! The apron is shorter
than ever," she said. "It's plain to me
now that sewing a narrow ruffle
on the bottom of an apron makes it shorter.

I'll remember that. I always say
you can learn something new every day
if you only use your head."

Many words have more than one meaning.

What part of a man do you mean
when you talk about his head?

What do you mean by the word **head**
when you talk about the head of a bed?

What is the other end of a bed called?

What do you mean by the word **head**
when you talk about the head of a pin?

What is the other end of a pin called?

What do you mean by the head
of a parade or the head of a line?

How many different meanings of the word
foot can you think of?

Which part of a stairway is called
the foot of the stairs? What part of a tree
is called the foot of it?

You know that the word **chop** means cut.

When a man says he chops down a tree,
you know he means that he cuts it down.

The word **chop** may also mean a kind
of food, such as a lamb chop.

Have you ever eaten lamb chops?

What other chops have you eaten?

Do you know a Chinese food
that has the word **chop** in its name?

The word **run** has many meanings
that you know and use.

When you run, you use your legs and
your feet to get from one place to another.

What does water do when it runs?

What does a watch do when it runs?

What would you do to run a rope
through a big ring?

What does a man do to run a car?

What do you mean by the word **run**
when you say that a road runs by a house?

What different meanings can you give
for each of these words?

spring   watch   trunk   box   match   light

Useful Endings

The ending **ful** is one that you will often find in your reading.

The word **careful** is made by adding the ending **ful** to the word **care**.

How is the word **useful** made?

When you are being careful, do you take some care, or no care at all?

Most birds are useful. Does that mean that they do some good or no good?

Look at each of the following words and be ready to tell how it is made:

helpful   thoughtful   handful   mouthful

Can a car be helpful? How?

Can a car be thoughtful? Why or why not?

Should you ever try to talk with a mouthful of food? Why not?

Is a handful of sand enough to fill a sandbox?

One of the most useful endings is **er**.
When the ending **er** is added to **farm,**
it makes the word **farmer.**

You know that a farmer is a man
who works on a farm or runs a farm.

How is the word **teacher** made?
What does a teacher do?

How is the word **banker** made?
Where does a banker work?
What does a banker do?

How is each of these words made?

reader   **printer**   **sleeper**   **player**
catcher   **waiter**   **keeper**   **painter**

How many meanings can you think of
for the word **reader**?

What does a printer do?

Is a catcher a ball player?

What does the keeper of a zoo do?

If you wanted someone to bring
your dinner to you, which one would
you ask, a painter, a sleeper, or a waiter?

Our Friend, the Catbird

Have you ever heard a bird that sounded
like a cat? There is a bird that can make
a noise just like the meow of a cat.
That bird is called the catbird.

The catbird doesn't always sound
like a cat. Often he makes real music.
He can also give the birdcalls
of other birds. Then you have to see
him to be sure that you hear a catbird.

A catbird seems to be all gray. However,
if you can get a good look at one, you
can see a black cap. Sometimes you
can see some red under the tail.

In the spring, mother and father catbird
look for a good place to build a nest.
They like to build their nest where it
can't be seen without looking for it.

The nest holds from three to six eggs. After the mother catbird has laid the eggs in the nest, the father catbird will sometimes take a turn sitting on them.

When the young catbirds have come from the eggs, there is a noisy time. The young birds call for food, and mother and father catbird work hard filling the wide mouths of their young.

Catbirds are curious about people. Often they will follow a man along a road just as if they want to find out where he is going.

They are curious about noises, too. If they hear a strange noise, they soon go to find out what is happening.

Catbirds make fine music all spring. They also eat things that might hurt gardens. That is why people like to have them around.

The Magic Glasses

One day the Little Old Woman was
working in her garden when a man came by.

On his back he carried a large bag
filled with things he wanted to sell.
He tapped on the gate.

"May I sell you something today?"
he asked. "I have a large number
of useful things. Do you need any pencils,
pins, scissors, matches, or string?

I also have some playthings. Would you
like balloons, kites, or toy scissors
to give to boys or girls?"

"No," said the Little Old Woman.
"I have very little money. It is all
I can do to buy enough to eat and drink."

"How about aprons, pans, or pails?"
he went on.

"No," she said. "I need my money to buy
the things I can't grow. Today I must go
to the store to get a loaf of bread and
some other things to eat. I can't buy
anything from you."

"How about some new glasses?" he asked.

"I don't need glasses,"
said the Little Old Woman.

"But these glasses are different,"
said the man. "They work like magic.
They make everything look ten times
as large as before."

"Why should I want things to look
ten times as large as before?" she asked.

"Why, the larger things are, the better
you can see them," he said.

"I've never thought of that," she said.
"But what you say must be true."

"Put the glasses on and see for yourself,"
said the man.

"I guess it won't hurt to try them,"
said the Little Old Woman slowly.
"But remember, I am not going to buy them."

"Just as you say," said the man.

He opened his bag and carefully took out
the magic glasses.   The Little Old Woman
put them on and looked at her garden.

She could hardly believe her eyes.
Her garden looked ten times as large
as before.

236

"How my garden has grown!"
cried the Little Old Woman.
"How plainly I can see everything!
This is a very fine pair of glasses!"

"I will sell them for very little money,"
said the man. "I am sure that they would
come in very handy."

It didn't take the Little Old Woman long
to make up her mind.

"That is just what I was thinking!"
she said. "Wait right here. I'll get
the money." She hurried into the house
and got the money for the pair of glasses
from her cooky jar.

After the man had gone, she said
to herself, "I should like to look
at the garden through these glasses again.
But first I must go to the store to buy
what I need."

Soon she was ready to go to the store. She said, "I will take the glasses with me and wear them while I am buying food. If I see things plainly, maybe I'll get more for my money."

So the Little Old Woman put the new pair of glasses into her pocket. When she got to the store, she put them on again.

"What fine rolls you have today!" she said to the storekeeper. "Each one is as large as a loaf of bread. I will buy one roll. I won't need a loaf of bread today."

The storekeeper got one roll for her.

"What large lamb chops you have today!"
she said. "One chop is almost as large as
a leg of lamb. I will need only one chop.
That will last me a long time."

The storekeeper got one lamb chop for her.

Then the storekeeper got some paper and
tied up the chop and the roll for her.

When the Little Old Woman got home,
she started to get her dinner.

First she looked at the roll. "This roll
is as big as a loaf of bread," she said,
"I will cut off a piece and
leave the rest for tomorrow."

After she had cut a piece off the roll,
she put the rest of it into her bread box.
Then she looked at the chop.

"This chop is also too large," she said.
"I will cut off a piece and leave the rest
for tomorrow."

So she cut a piece off the chop and
put away the rest of it for the next day.

When her lamb chop was done,
the Little Old Woman buttered the piece
of roll. She took off her glasses
and put them away carefully.
Then she sat down to eat her dinner.

She looked at the piece of buttered roll.
It looked very small. She looked
at the piece she had cut from the lamb chop.
It looked very small, too.

"Well!" she said. "What has happened
to my dinner? This won't fill me up.
There is not enough here to feed a goldfish."

She began to look around because she
thought part of her dinner was gone.

She looked under the dishes. She even
looked under her chair. But she couldn't
find any more food.

"This is very strange!" she said.
"Something must be wrong!"

The Little Old Woman looked all around
again. Then she said, "I must use my head
to find out what happened to the rest
of my dinner. I'm sure it hasn't gone far."

So she tied a wet rag around her head
and touched the tip of her first finger
to her nose. Then she shut her eyes
and thought and thought.

Soon she knew what to do.

"What a silly old woman I am!" she said.
"How can I find my dinner when I can't see
plainly? I must put on my new pair
of glasses!"

The Little Old Woman got her new glasses and put them on. Then she started to look for her dinner. She didn't have to look far. There it was, as plain as it could be, right on the table.

As she began to eat her dinner, she said, "I was very wise to put on my new glasses. Now I see my dinner very plainly. What a fine big dinner it is! Now I'm afraid I can't eat all of it!"

Cutting Up

When I can't go outdoors to play,
My scissors pass the time away.
My scissors cut out what I wish —
A crocodile, an owl, a fish.

I like to cut out little zoos
With zebras, monkeys, kangaroos.
I have a sheep, a horse, a calf,
An ostrich, and a big giraffe.

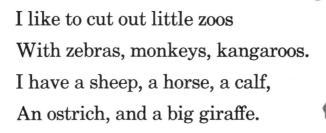

Soon I'll have a big parade
Of circus horses that I've made.
What fun to see them passing by,
Gayly trotting, heads up high!

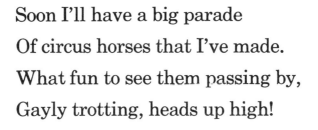

Now I am sure that you can see
What fun my scissors give to me.
And now you know what mine can do,
Why not get out your scissors, too?

243

The Dog and His Bone

Once there was a dog that liked bones
very much. He liked bones so much that
he did nothing all day long but look
for bones.

One day he was taking home a bone which
he had found. Everything went well
until he came to a bridge.

There was a hole between two boards
on the bridge. Through the hole he
could see the water. In the water he saw
himself and his bone. He thought he
was seeing another dog with a big bone.

The dog pushed himself through the hole between the boards.   One bone was not enough for him.   He wanted both bones. Into the water he fell.   And as he fell, he let go of his bone.

Quickly he put his head under the water to get back his bone.   He couldn't find it. Then he looked around for the other dog and the other bone.   He couldn't find them.

Now the silly dog had no bone at all. He kept putting his head as far under the water as he could, trying to find his own bone.   Still he couldn't find it.

At last two boys came across the bridge. They saw that the silly dog was about to drown.   Between them they pulled the dog to land.

Sometimes it is better to be happy with what you have than to want more.

Working with Words

Take **w** away from **wide**.

Put in **sl** to make **slide**.

Let's make a wide slide.

We can make a wide slide on the hill by the fire station.

Add **pl** to **ate**. Now you have **plate**.

We used paper plates when we ate at the picnic on Saturday.

Add **d** to **ate**. Now you have **date**.

We ate the dates my uncle gave us.

Take **p** away from **pin**.

Put in **th** and you have **thin**.

Have you ever seen anyone as thin as a pin?

Shut and **sheep** begin with the sound of **sh**. Listen for the sound of **sh** as you say **shut** and **sheep**. Shut the gate and keep the sheep out of the garden.

Often you can learn a new word
by using good sense and the beginning sound
of the new word.

Try it on the words with very black letters
in the following lines. Some of those words
may be new to you.

One **rainy** day Eddie's mother had to go
to the post office to mail a letter
she had **written**. She asked Eddie to look
after the house while she was gone.

Eddie likes to make up stories
about things that never happen. He **decided**
that it would be fun to tell his mother
a story when she returned home!

When Eddie's mother got home, she asked
him **whether** anyone had called. Eddie
said, "A clown came to the door and asked
for a glass of water to **cure** his hiccups!"

"Did that cure them?" asked his mother.

"No, it didn't," **replied** Eddie. "Then we

tried other things. He jumped ten times without stopping. That did no good.

"Then he held his **breath** for as long as he could. He still had the hiccups.

"Next I gave him some **crackers** to eat. Even that didn't **fix** them.

"The fifth thing he tried was a real circus **stunt**. He turned somersaults, but that didn't work.

"**Finally** he said he'd try running, and he ran right down the street and didn't come back!"

Eddie's mother had been listening with a smile on her face. "What did this clown look like?" she asked.

"Well," said Eddie, "he had on a violet-colored hat, and he **wore** large green mittens!"

"Why, I saw him too," said Eddie's mother. "He ran **past** me as I came up the street."

Eddie didn't know what to think. Do you?

Look at these pairs of words.

dirty   **funny**   **lucky**   **silly**
dirtier   **funnier**   **luckier**   **sillier**

When the ending **er** is added
to some words ending in **y**, **i** is used
in place of the **y**.

Now look at these pairs of words.

handy   **tricky**   **sleepy**   **tidy**
handiest **trickiest** **sleepiest** **tidiest**

When the ending **est** is added
to some words ending in **y**, **i** is used
in place of the **y**.

What word was used in making each
of the following words? What letter
was used in place of **y**? What letters
were added?

angrier **hungrier** **merrier** **prettier**
happiest **silliest**   **merriest** **prettiest**

249

In many words **i** is used in place of **y** before the ending **es**.

Look at the word **puppies**. Take off the ending **es**. Now put **y** in place of the **i**, and you have **puppy**.

What word was used to make each of the following words? What letter was used in place of **y**? What letters were added?

cookies   ladies   parties   stories

Look at the words **carry** and **carried**. When the ending **ed** is added to some words ending in **y**, **i** is used in place of the **y**.

What word does **cried** come from? Take off the ending **ed**. Put **y** in place of the **i**, and you have **cry**.

Start with **hurried**. Take off the ending **ed**. Put **y** in place of the **i**, and you have **hurry**.

Take the ending **ed** from the word **tried**. Put **y** in place of the **i**, and you have **try**.

When you say the words **wave, race,**
and **rope**, you cannot hear the sound of **e**
at the end of the words.

Do you know why the **e** at the end
of such words is called **silent e**?

When **ing** is added to words like **wave,**
race, and **rope**, the **e** is taken off
before the **ing** is added.

The words **waving, racing,** and **roping**
are made from **wave, race,** and **rope**.

How are these words made?

coming　　**facing**　　**firing**　　**giving**

When **er** is added to words like **make,**
ride, and **mine**, the **e** is taken off
before the **er** is added. The words **maker,**
rider, and **miner** are made in this way.
How are these words made?

juggler　　**dancer**　　**joker**　　**user**

251

Words Made by Adding *ly*

Look at the word **slowly**. It is made by adding the ending **ly** to the word **slow**.

The word **lately** is made by adding the ending **ly** to the word **late**.

How were the following words made?

queerly   **plainly**   **patiently**   **quietly**

Look at the word **hungrily**. It is made by putting **i** in place of the **y** in **hungry** and adding **ly**.

The word **luckily** is made by putting **i** in place of the **y** in **lucky** and adding **ly**.

How were the following words made?

merrily   **angrily**   **prettily**   **happily**

What words in the following lines end in **ly**?

This dog that will gladly do all kinds of tricks
Has cleverly learned how to count up to six.
He lately has learned on his hind legs
    to walk,
And now he is merrily learning to talk.

Adding a Letter Before the Ending

Do you see the word **tap** in **tapped**?

How many **p's** are in **tap**?

How many **p's** are in **tapped**?

To make **tapped**, begin with **tap**.
Add another **p** and the ending **ed**.

To make **sitting**, begin with **sit**.
Add another **t** and the ending **ing**.

Tell how the words in *The Race* which have
very black letters were made.

The Race

Three little rabbits were **running** a race —
  And each of them hoped to be **winner**;
Two of the **runners hopped** better by far
  Than the third, who was just a **beginner**.
The first one **stepped** into a very deep hole;
  The second **stopped** off to eat dinner.
The third one kept **hopping** and jumping
    along,
  And **topped** both his friends as the **winner**.

253

VOCABULARY

ON WE GO is planned to follow the first book for the second year, COME ALONG. It repeats each word in the vocabulary of COME ALONG, except some proper names. The names of characters in ON WE GO are not counted as new words unless the names are also used as meaningful words. The following list contains the 216 new words introduced in ON WE GO. Variants formed by adding the ending *s, es, d, ed, ing, er, est, y,* or *ly* to words previously taught, and compounds formed by joining two word forms previously taught are not counted as new words. Variants formed by adding *n* or *en,* the prefix *un,* or the suffix *ful* are counted as new words until special lessons teaching the formation of such words are reached in the text. The list does not include words which are used for practice in the special lessons for developing the power to unlock words independently.

5. Noodle	I've	ground	82. ——
short	28. oatmeal	52. coach	83. ——
6. dig	stay	golden	84. ——
garden	29. kitchen	53. footmen	85. ——
7. bone	pan	(man)	86. ——
tail	30. drink	princess	87. hurdy-gurdy
8. hole	toast	54. hill	spring
wings	31. goldfish	live	88. ragged
9. fairy	between	55. pretty	woman
wagging	32. quickly	56. ate	89. politely
10. shape	33. finished	side	sell
size	34. Indians	57. ——	90. bread
11. pitter	read	58. rode	smelled
patter	35. ——	59. ——	91. neat
12. fine	36. Sally	60. ——	tidy
question	37. ——	61. ——	92. gay
13. best	38. bakery	62. ——	park
14. answered	flowers	63. ——	93. through
15. Miss	39. ——	64. ——	94. chair
trotted	40. ——	65. ——	fresh
16. dinner	41. ——	66. ——	95. sit
giraffe	42. different	67. ——	96. music
17. neck	43. ——	68. ——	often
18. hungry	44. pieces	69. ——	97. leave
19. ——	started	70. ——	queer
20. ——	45. cookies	71. ——	98. handle
21. ——	gingerbread	72. ——	round
22. ——	46. batter	73. ——	99. merry
23. mumps	eyes	74. ——	100. dance
24. Bob	47. climb	75. ——	ring
you'll	hair	76. ——	101. bell
25. breakfast	48. fell	77. ——	teacher
twice	49. covered	78. ——	102. such
26. care	50. apples	79. ——	mayor
stairs	near	80. ——	103. ——
27. cocoa	51. cat	81. ——	104. ——

105. also
fathers
106. ——
107. ——
108. ——
109. picnic
sand-
wiches
110. ——
111. ——
112. ——
113. seemed
wise
114. small
wife
115. build
doesn't
116. larger
promise
117. barn
grow
118. dirty
floor
119. knocked
poor
120. food
nose
121. hasn't
122. sheep
unhappy
123. broken
patient
124. butter
feed
125. fill
last
126. slowly
127. rest
128. return
129. ——
130. ——
131. magic
washed
132. ——
133. ——
134. hose
wand
135. tapped
waved
136. robe

trunk
137. mind
138. ——
139. fence
gray
140. Chinese
141. dragon
142. blow
143. pet
wrong
144. frightened
loud
145. ears
hind
146. feel
friend
147. careful
noise
148. shouted
149. ——
150. most
quiet
151. slept
152. bowed
hello
153. ——
154, ——
155. ——
156. ——
157. ——
158. ——
159. ——
160. middle
listen
161. mean
162. ——
163. ——
164. ——
165. ——
166. ——
167. ——
168. ——
169. ——
170. ——
171. ——
172. ——
173. ——
174. ——
175. ——
176. ——

177. ——
178. ——
179. ——
180. ——
181. ——
182. ——
183. ——
184. ——
185. ——
186. ——
187. ——
188. ——
189. clown
island
190. juggle
somersaults
191. card
report
192. jokes
193. pass
tests
194. whole
world
195. beard
ten
196. Monday
Thursday
197. loaf
puffs
198. clever
199. lucky
Tuesday
200. ——
201. late
young
202. dear
oh
203. flew
hen
204. Wednesday
205. ——
206. twelve
207. nest
rolled
208. eggs
laid
209. paper
step
210. ——
211. carpet

212. pins
213. ——
214. ——
215. ——
216. ——
217. ——
218. ——
219. fingers
touched
220. shut
tied
221. cloth
plain
222. pair
wide
223. narrow
sew
224. ——
225. scissors
ruffle
226. ——
227. ——
228. chop
229. ——
230. ——
231. ——
232. ——
233. ——
234. ——
235. ——
236. ——
237. ——
238. ——
239. ——
240. ——
241. ——
242. ——
243. ——
244. ——
245. ——
246. ——
247. ——
248. ——
249. ——
250. ——
251. ——
252. ——
253. ——

ACKNOWLEDGMENTS

Grateful acknowledgment is made to the following publishers and authors for permission to adapt and use copyrighted material:

To Story Parade, Inc. for permission to adapt the following stories: "Home with the Mumps" by Earl Marvin Rush, copyright 1942, and "The Boy Who Owned an Elephant" by Malvin Wald, copyright 1947.

To Albert Whitman and Company for permission to adapt *Snipp, Snapp, Snurr and the Gingerbread* by Maj Lindman, copyright 1939.

To The Macmillan Company for permission to adapt the story "The Seven White Cats" from the book *The Blue Teapot* by Alice Dalgliesh, copyright 1931.

To the Oxford University Press for permission to adapt *The Hurdy Gurdy Man* by Margery Bianco, copyright 1933.

To Coward-McCann, Inc. for permission to publish the story "Oswald Makes Magic," which is based on *Oswald's Pet Dragon* by Carl Glick, copyright 1943 by Coward-McCann, Inc.

To Henry Holt and Company for permission to adapt *Eemi: The Story of a Clown* by Frances Duncombe, copyright 1946.

To Thomas Nelson and Sons for permission to adapt Chapters 7 and 9 of *The Little Old Woman Who Used Her Head* by Hope Newell, copyright 1935.

The illustrations for "Noodle," "The Queer Apron," "The Magic Glasses," and pages 4 and 187 were made by Albert D. and Violet Jousset; those for "Home with the Mumps," "Snipp and His Brothers," and pages 1 and 3 by Mary Stevens; those for "The Seven White Cats" and pages 65, 84, 158, 159, 164, 217, 232, 233, 243, 244, and 245 by Sally Tate; those for "The Hurdy-Gurdy Man" and page 86 by C. L. Hartman; those for "Oswald Makes Magic" by Katherine Elgin; those for "Bob's Elephant" by Harry Lees; those for "Room Enough," "The Story of a Clown," and pages 85 and 188 by Leon Berthold; and those for pages 252 and 253 by Bruno Frost.